EYEWITNESS BOOKS

ROCKS & MINERALS

Slice from
septarian knob

Garnet-chlorite schist

Cinnabar

Hematite

Granite

Gypsum desert rose

Wenlock limestone
with trilobite fossils

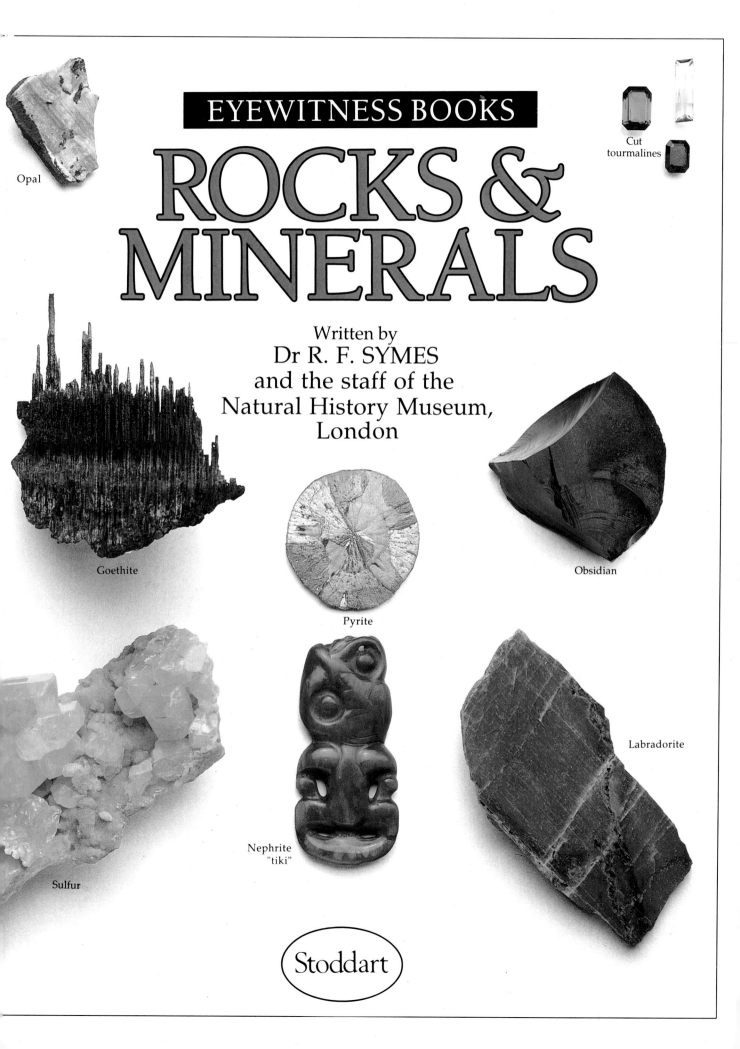

Opal

EYEWITNESS BOOKS

ROCKS & MINERALS

Cut
tourmalines

Written by
Dr R. F. SYMES
and the staff of the
Natural History Museum,
London

Goethite

Pyrite

Obsidian

Sulfur

Nephrite
"tiki"

Labradorite

Stoddart

Magnifying lens

DK

A DORLING KINDERSLEY BOOK

This Eyewitness Book has been
conceived by Dorling Kindersley Limited
and Editions Gallimard

Mixed rough
and polished
pebbles

Project editor Janice Lacock
Art editor Neville Graham
Managing art editor Jane Owen
Special photography
Colin Keates (Natural History Museum, London)
and Andreas Einsiedel
Editorial consultants
Dr R. F. Symes (Natural History Museum, London)
and Dr Wendy Kirk (University College, London)

Copyright © 1988 by Dorling Kindersley

First published in 1988 by
STODDART PUBLISHING CO. LIMITED
34 Lesmill Road
Toronto, Canada
M3B 2T6

Reprinted 1995, 1997

First published in the United Kingdom by
Dorling Kindersley

Canadian Cataloguing in Publication Data
Main entry under title:
Rocks & minerals
(Eyewitness series)
Includes index.
ISBN 0-7737-2704-3

1. Rocks – Juvenile literature. 2. Mineralogy –
Juvenile literature. I. Series.

QE432.2.R62 1988   j552   C88-093216-3

Colour reproduction by Colourscan, Singapore
Typeset by Windsorgraphics, Ringwood, Hampshire
Printed in Singapore by Toppan Printing Co. (S) Pte Ltd.

Chisel

Geologist's hammer

Chalcedony cameo

Contents

Cut citrine

Baryte
desert rose

Clear topaz

Cut amethyst

The Earth

Early view of Earth with a central fire

ONE OF THE NINE known planets that revolve around the Sun, the Earth is thought to be about 4.6 billion years old. Geology is the study of the history of the Earth. Because rocks can provide valuable information about the Earth in previous times, geologists study them and work out the processes and events that produced them. As we can currently bore only a few miles into the crust, or outer shell, we cannot sample rocks from the mantle (the inner shell) directly. The rocks and minerals shown here come from many locations and introduce important features that are explained in more detail later in the book.

PRECIOUS METALS
Platinum, silver, and gold are rare and valuable metals. *For more information, see pages 58-59.*

SEASHORE PEBBLES
These are formed by the weathering of larger rocks by wave action. *For more information, see pages 14-15.*

Gold in quartz vein

CRYSTAL HABITS
The shape and size of a crystal is known as its habit. *For more information, see pages 46-47.*

Cubes of pyrite

MINERAL ORES
These are the source of most useful metals. *For more information, see pages 56-57.*

Cut citrine, a variety of quartz

Cassiterite (tin ore) from Bolivia

Diamond in kimberlite

THE STRUCTURE OF THE EARTH
The Earth consists of three major parts: the core, the mantle, and the crust. The crust and upper mantle form continental and oceanic "plates" that move slowly over the mantle beneath. The closer to the center of the Earth, the greater the temperature and pressure.

Crust, 4-44 miles (6-70 km) thick

Solid mantle, approximately 1,800 miles (2,900 km) thick

Molten outer core, approximately 1,430 miles (2,300 km) thick

Solid inner core, approximately 750 miles (1,200 km) radius

GEMSTONES
Rare, hard-wearing, and attractive minerals may be cut as gemstones. They are used mainly in jewelry. *For more information, see pages 50-55.*

Quartz crystals from France

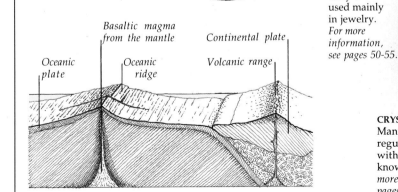

Basaltic magma from the mantle

Continental plate

Oceanic plate

Oceanic ridge

Volcanic range

CRYSTALS
Many minerals form regular-shaped solids with flat surfaces, known as crystals. *For more information, see pages 44-47.*

Shelly limestone

MOVING PLATES
Where plates collide, mountain ranges like the Himalayas may form. In the ocean, material from the mantle fills the gap between plates to form a ridge. In other areas, oceanic plates are forced down beneath continental plates, causing volcanic activity.

FOSSILS
These rocks contain the remains of, or impressions made by, former plants or animals. *For more information, see pages 38-39.*

Quartzite
beach
pebbles

IGNEOUS ROCKS
The most common types
of rocks have formed
from molten magma.
*For more information,
see pages 16-17.*

Granite

— Delta
— Suez Canal
— City of Cairo

— Nile River

**SATELLITE PICTURE OF
NILE RIVER AND DELTA**
The Nile River carries
rock debris eroded from
rocks in central Egypt
and deposits it in the
delta and the sea,
where it may eventu-
ally form sedimentary
rocks (pp. 11 and 20).

VOLCANIC ROCKS
Volcanic activity
produces a number of
different types of rocks
and lava. *For more in-
formation, see pages 18-19.*

Hawaiian
ropy lava

Carboniferous
Limestone

Lake Amboseli, a dry lake

*Ingito Hills on edge of
East African Rift Valley*

Chyulu mountain range, Kenya

SEDIMENTARY ROCKS
These have formed from sediment that's been created by
the erosion of other rocks
and packed together.
*For more information,
see pages 20-23.*

Anthracite, the
hardest form of coal

Mount Meru   *Mount
Kilimanjaro*   *Pangani
River valley*   *Glaciers
of Kibo*

COAL
A sedimentary rock, coal has formed from
the fossilized remains of plants.
For more information, see pages 36-37.

SATELLITE PICTURE OF EAST AFRICA
This area shows a range of landscapes, formed from different
rocks. For example, volcanic rocks (p. 18) forming volcanic
Mount Kilimanjaro, and evaporites (p. 21) in dried-up lakes.

What are rocks and minerals?

James Hutton (1726-97), one of the founders of modern geology

Rocks ARE NATURAL AGGREGATES or combinations of one or more minerals. Some rocks, such as quartzite (pure quartz) and marble (pure calcite), contain only one mineral. Most, however, consist of more than one kind. Minerals are inorganic (nonliving) solids that are found in nature. They are made of elements such as silicon, oxygen, carbon, and iron. Here, two common rocks - granite and basalt - are shown with individual specimens of the major minerals of which they are formed. Rock-forming minerals can be divided into several groups - these are described in more detail on pages 42-43.

GRANITE AND ITS MAJOR MINERALS

Usually, several kinds of minerals are present in a rock, their size and texture varying according to how the rock formed. In granite, a coarse-grained, igneous rock, the three major minerals are visible to the naked eye. They are quartz (gray areas), feldspars (pink and white),and mica (black).

Quartz | Mica

Feldspar

BASALT AND ITS MAJOR MINERALS

Basalt consists mainly of three minerals - olivine, pyroxene, and plagioclase feldspar. But because it is fine-grained, it is not always possible to tell them apart with the naked eye. This olivine basalt is from the crater of the Kilauea volcano in Hawaii.

1 OLIVINE

Transparent green crystals of olivine are comparatively rare, and are known as peridot (p. 54).

2 FELDSPA

Flat or polishe crystals o labradorite, plagioclas feldspar fro Labrador, Canad display beautiful pla of color

Iridescer blue an orange visib on the surfac

Etched face

1 QUARTZ

Well-developed quartz crystals, like this group, may have milky, etched faces.

Augite crystal

Rock matrix

3 PYROXEN

This well developed, sing black crystal of augite (pyroxene) comes from Italy Augite crystals are found i various igneous rock

2 MICA

Black biotite (a type of mica) crystals can be split into wafer-thin sheets.

3 FELDSPAR

Crystals of orthoclase (a feldspar) may be milky white or pale pink.

The scope of rock forms

Rocks and minerals occur in many different forms. Rocks do not necessarily have to be hard and resistant; loose sand and wet clay are considered to be rocks. The individual size of minerals in a rock ranges from millimeters, in a fine-grained volcanic rock, to several yards in a granite pegmatite.

ROCKS FORMED WITHIN ROCKS
This sedimentary rock specimen is a claystone septarian nodule. Nodules (knobs) such as this are formed when groundwater redistributes minerals within a rock in a particular pattern. Nodules are sometimes known as concretions. Here, the pattern of veins is formed of calcite.

CRYSTALS FROM MINERAL ORE
Orange-red crystals of the mineral wulfenite from Arizona are formed in veins that carry lead and molybdenum.

ROCKS FORMED BY EVAPORATION
Stalactites are formed from substances that are deposited when dripping water evaporates (p. 22). This spectacular pale blue stalactite is composed entirely of the mineral chalcanthite (copper sulfate) and formed from copper-rich waters in a mine.

Section of a mine roof colored with deposits of the copper mineral, chalcanthite

Eruption of Mount Pelée, Martinique, on August 5, 1851

ROCKS FROM VOLCANIC ERUPTION
Despite its extraordinary appearance, "Pele's hair" is technically a rock. It consists of golden-brown hairlike fibers of basalt glass that sometimes enclose tiny olivine crystals, and was formed from the eruption of basaltic magma as a lava spray.

Lighter bands of pyroxene and plagioclase feldspar

Dark layer of chromite

ROCKS THAT FORM IN LAYERS
Norite is an igneous rock composed of the minerals pyroxene, plagioclase feldspar, and the chromium-rich mineral chromite. In this specimen from South Africa, the dark and light minerals have separated from each other so that the rock is layered. The dark chromite layers are an important source of chromium.

How rocks are formed

GEOLOGICAL PROCESSES work in constant cycles - redistributing the chemical elements, minerals, and rocks within and at the surface of the Earth. The processes that occur within the Earth, such as metamorphism (changing) and mountain building, are driven by the Earth's internal heat. Surface processes, such as weathering, are activated by the Sun's energy.

Andesite formed from a volcanic eruption in the Solomon Islands in the Pacific

Pure quartz sand formed from weathered granite or sandstone

VOLCANIC ACTIVITY
When rocks of the crust and upper mantle melt, they form magma that may be extruded, or forced out, at the Earth's surface by volcanic activity. The resulting rocks are extrusive igneous rocks (p. 16). The most common example is basalt.

Basaltic lava from a lava flow in Hawaii

VOLCANIC LANDMARK
Le Puy de Dôme, France, is a plug that was once the central core of an ancient volcano.

Gabbro, the coarse-grained equivalent of basalt, from Finland

IGNEOUS ROCKS
Sugar Loaf Mountain, Brazil, consists of intrusive igneous rocks that have gradually reached the surface when rocks covering them were weathered away.

Volcanic activity Weathering

Surface

Igneous rocks

Melting

Magma

Migmatite from Finland

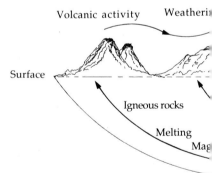

Granite, containing large crystals of pink feldspar, from northern England

ROCKS FROM MAGMA
Rocks formed within the Earth from molten magma are called intrusive igneous rocks (p. 16). They are also known as plutonic, after Pluto, the Greek god of the underworld. One such rock, granite, can form enormous masses called batholiths in mountain belts.

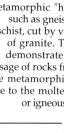

MELTING *right*
Occasionally, high temperatures and pressures cause rocks to partially melt. If the rock is then squeezed, snake-like veins may form. Migmatites are mixed rocks consisting of a metamorphic "host" such as gneiss or schist, cut by veins of granite. They demonstrate the passage of rocks from the metamorphic state to the molten or igneous.

When the weather acts on rocks it may lead to chemical changes or cause the rocks to fragment (p. 12) and form sediments. For example, sand grains are produced when quartz-bearing rocks are broken down, and clays form from weathered rocks full of feldspar.

Clays produced by weathering become important parts of soils

DEPOSIT OF SEDIMENTS

Sediments are carried by rivers, or by the wind in desert regions. When the wind or water slows down as, when a river runs into a lake, the sediment is deposited into layers of different sized particles. When these are compacted (pressed) together they form sedimentary rocks (p. 20).

Layered sandstone from Arkansas

RIVER TRANSPORT

Rivers such as these (seen from space) carry rock fragments from one area to another. The Mississippi alone deposits thousands of tons of debris into its delta each day.

Banded claystone from Uganda, East Africa

THE ROCK CYCLE

There is no starting point in this cycle which has been going on for millions of years.

Transport

Deposition

Heat and pressure

Sedimentary rocks

Metamorphic rocks

200-million-year-old desert sandstone from Scotland

METAMORPHIC ROCKS

Quartz veins stand out in this schist rock face in Scotland. The area contains many metamorphic rocks.

Quartzite, an altered sandstone, formed by pressure beneath the Earth's surface

Granite

Gneiss

Gneiss, a banded metamorphic rock

Mica schist formed from metamorphosed claystones

METAMORPHISM

The deeper a rock is within the Earth, the greater the pressure exerted on it from the rocks above it, and the higher the temperature. Pressure and heat cause the rocks to change or "metamorphose" as the minerals recrystallize. The new rocks are called metamorphic rocks (p. 24).

Weathering and erosion

ALL ROCKS BREAK DOWN at the Earth's surface. Weathering is mainly a chemical reaction, aided by the presence of water. Rocks are also broken down by mechanical processes involving rain, alternate freezing and thawing, the abrasive (scraping) action of sediment in water, wind and, ice.

Wind erosion

Constant attack by sediment in wind may slowly grind away at a rock and erode it.

MONUMENT VALLEY, ARIZONA
Large-scale abrasion by the wind produces huge, protruding landforms called buttes.

ABRASION BY THE WIND
The abrasive action of the wind wears away softer layers of rock and leaves the harder ones sticking out, as in this desert rock from East Africa.

SAND BLASTING
Faceted desert pebbles, formed by sand constantly being blown against them, are called dreikanters.

Weathering caused by temperature changes

Rock expands and contracts as the temperature changes, causing it to break up. Shattering is also caused when water in the rock freezes and expands.

Sandstone composed of sand collected 200 million years ago in a desert environment

Sand from a present-day desert in Saudi Arabia

DESERT EROSION
Rocks formed in desert conditions, where sediment is carried by wind, are often reddish in color and composed of characteristically rounded sand grains.

DESERT ENVIRONMENT
Wind and temperature changes cause continual weathering and bizarre, barren landscapes in the Sahara Desert.

ONION-SKIN WEATHERING
In this type of weathering, changes i temperature cause the surface layers of rock to expand, contract, and fina peel away from the underlying rock.

Fine-grain doleri

Onion-sk weathere doler

Peel lay like on skins, cau by changes temperati

Chemical weathering

nly a few minerals can sist weathering by inwater, which is a eak acid. Minerals ssolved at the surface ay be carried down and deposited in the soil d rock below.

Fresh, unaltered granite

Coarse, weathered granite

ALTERED MINERALS
Granite is split by the expansion of water as it freezes. Its minerals are then chemically altered, producing coarse rock fragments.

GRANITE TORS
Tors, weathered rounded rocks, are formed of the remains left when the surrounding rocks have been eroded away. This example is on Dartmoor, England.

ossan altered by undwater

Secondary minerals

CHEMICAL CHANGES
Chemical weathering of an ore vein may cause redistribution of minerals. The bright-colored minerals were formed from deposits of minerals that dissolved from rocks at higher levels. They are called secondary deposits.

TROPICAL WEATHERING
In certain tropical climates, quartz is dissolved and carried away, while feldspars are altered to clay minerals that may collect on the surface as a thick deposit of bauxite (p. 56).

Ice erosion

As glaciers move they pick up fragments of rock which become frozen into the base of the ice. The moving, frozen mass causes further erosion of underlying rocks.

Large rock fragment

Scratches caused by a glacier

RTHENON, ATHENS, GREECE
emicals in the air can react with stone and use drastic weathering. This can be seen on Parthenon and on gargoyles on buildings.

MORTERATSCH GLACIER, SWITZERLAND *left*
Glaciers are a major cause of erosion in mountainous regions.

SCRATCHED ROCK
The deep gouge marks on this limestone from Grindelwald, Switzerland, were caused by abrasive rock fragments contained in the glacier that flowed over it.

GLACIER DEPOSITS
A till is a deposit left by a melting glacier and contains crushed rock fragments ranging from microscopic grains to large pebbles. Ancient tills that have become packed into hard rock are called tillite. This specimen is from the Flinders Range in South Australia, which was covered with glaciers some 600 million years ago.

Rocks on the seashore

At THE SEASHORE, geological processes can be seen taking place. Many seashores are backed by cliffs, beneath which is a deposit of coarse material that has fallen from above. This is gradually broken up by the sea and sorted into pebbles, gravel, sand, and mud. Then the various sizes of sediment are deposited separately - this is the raw material for future sedimentary rocks (p. 20).

Pebbles on Chesil Beach, England

GRADED GRAINS
On the beach, these pebbles are sorted by wave and tide action. The sand comes from a nearby area. It is pure quartz; the other rock-forming minerals were washed away by constant wave movement.

Large, coarse pebbles

Mica schist

Irregularly shaped pyrite nodule

SKIMMING STONES
As every schoolchild knows, the best stones for skimming are disk-shaped. They are most likely to be sedimentary or metamorphic rocks, since these split easily into sheets.

Slates

HIDDEN CRYSTALS
Pyrite nodules are common in chalk areas. They may develop interesting shapes. The dull outside breaks to reveal unexpected, radiating crystals inside.

LOCAL STONES
These pebbles reflect the local geology, all coming from the rocks of the immediate neighborhood of the beach where they were collected. They are metamorphic rocks that have been worn into flat disks.

SHELLY PEBBLES
Empty sea shells are subjected to continuous wave action. In time, the sharp edges of broken shells may become smoothed and form pebbles. These are from a beach in New Zealand.

PRESERVED WAVES
Ripple marks and other similar structures form under water from sand carried by currents and can be seen on many beaches at low tide. In this specimen from Finland, ripple marks are preserved in sandstone, showing that the same sedimentary processes have been going on for millions of years (p. 20).

AMBER PEBBLES
Amber is the fossil resin of extinct cone-bearing trees that lived thousands of years ago. It is especially common along the Baltic coasts of Russia and Poland.

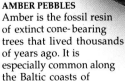

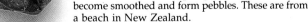

areas of volcanic activity, beach
d may contain dark minerals and
n no quartz. The olivine sand
es from Raasay, Scotland; the
gnetite-bearing sand is from
erife, an island off the
thwest coast of Africa.

Dark olivine sand

Magnetite-bearing sand

Black volcanic ash beach on north
coast of Santorini, Greece

Medium-size coarse pebbles

Small, fine pebbles

Finest pebbles

Quartz sand

DISCOVERED IN CHALK

Because flint nodules are hard,
they resist abrasion (scraping)
and can be seen on
beaches in Chalk areas,
such as those below
the famous White
Cliffs of Dover, England.

Chalk cliffs often produce pyrite
and flint nodules

*Smooth,
yellowish
exterior*

*Glistening crystals
radiate outward*

Flint nodules (knobs) from below Chalk cliffs

GRANITIC ORIGIN

In granite country,
beach pebbles tend to
be of quartz, (an
abundant vein
mineral) or pink
or gray granite.

FOREIGN
MATERIAL

Not all beach
rocks are from
local areas.
This
porphyritic
igneous
rock was
probably
carried across
the North Sea
from Norway
to England
by ice during
the last Ice Age,
c. 18,000 B.C.

Assorted glass pebbles

Brick pebble

SYNTHETIC PEBBLES

Apart from the usual natural minerals and rocks, man-made
objects may be washed ashore, possibly from ships, or
dumped on the beach. Some of them may eventually become
rounded by wave action.

PROTECTING THE BEACH

Man-made jetties keep pebbles
and sand from drifting.

Igneous rocks

Basalt needle, St. Helena

Tʜᴇsᴇ ʀᴏᴄᴋs are formed when molten magma from deep within the Earth's crust and upper mantle (p. 6) cools and solidifies (hardens). There are two types: intrusive and extrusive. Intrusive rocks solidify within the Earth's crust and only appear at the surface after the rocks above them have eroded away. Extrusive rocks are formed when magma erupts from a volcano as lava, then cools at the surface.

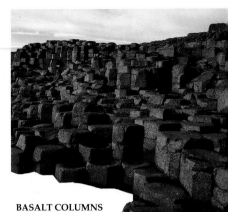

BASALT COLUMNS
When basaltic lava cools, it often forms hexagonal columns. This spectacular example the Giant's Causeway in Northern Ireland.

Biotite granite

Graphic granite

Pink gran

Black grains are biotite, a form of mica (p. 42)

Long, angular quartz crystals look like ancient writing against the larger pale pink feldspar crystals

Pink coloring due to t high level of potassiu feldspar in the ro

GRANITE
A very common intrusive rock, granite consists mainly of coarse grains of quartz, feldspar, and mica (p. 8). The individual grains are large because they formed as the magma cooled slowly deep in the earth. Granite is usually speckled and varies in color from gray to red according to the different amounts of minerals. Granite is found in many parts of the world. The biotite granite shown here comes from Hay Tor, an outcrop at the highest point on Dartmoor in southwest England (p. 13).

PITCHSTONE
Formed when volcanic lava cools very quickly, pitchstone contains some small crystals of feldspar and quartz and has a dull, resin-like appearance. Pitchstone may be brown, black, or gray, and large crystals of feldspar and quartz are sometimes visible.

OBSIDIAN
Like pitchstone, obsidian is a glass formed from rapidly cooled lava. It forms so quickly that there is no time for crystals to grow. The sharp edges shown on this sample from Iceland are characteristic of obsidian, hence its use as an early tool (p. 29).

Pyroxene

Olivine

Plagioclase
feldspar

GABBRO
An intrusive rock, gabbro consists of dark minerals such as olivine and augite. It has coarse grains, as large crystals formed when the magma slowly cooled. This sample is from the Isle of Skye, Scotland.

Phenocryst of feldspar

FELDSPAR PORPHYRY
Porphyries are rocks that contain large crystals called phenocrysts within a medium-grained rock. This particular sample contains feldspar crystals and comes from Wales.

THIN SECTION OF GABBRO
When a very thin slice of rock is viewed under a microscope using a particular kind of light, hidden features, such as crystal shape, are revealed (p. 42). Here, the highly colored grains are minerals called olivine and pyroxene, and the gray mineral is plagioclase feldspar.

Vesicular basalt

Empty vesicles
or holes

Amygdaloidal
basalt

BASALT
Formed from hardened lava, basalt is the most common extrusive rock. It is similar in composition to gabbro but has finer grains. When the lava cools, it may split into many-sided columns. Among the most well known of these spectacular structures are the Needle on St. Helena, an island in the Atlantic, and the Giant's Causeway in Ireland.

Hole filled
with calcite

**VESICULAR
VOLCANIC ROCKS**
Both rocks are basalts that were formed when bubbles of gas were trapped in hot lava scum. The vesicular basalt is light and full of holes known as vesicles. In amygdaloidal basalt, the holes were later filled in with minerals such as calcite. These rocks were collected from Hawaii, an area of great volcanic activity.

PERIDOTITE
A dark, heavy rock mainly containing minerals called olivine and pyroxene, peridotite is presumed to lie under layers of gabbro six miles (10 km) beneath the ocean floor. This sample was found in Odenwald, West Germany.

Green olivine crystals

Dark pyroxene crystals

Calcite vein

SERPENTINITE
As its name suggests, the dominant mineral in this coarse-grained red and green rock is serpentine. It is streaked with white veins of calcite. Serpentinite is common in the Alps.

Volcanic rocks

Ejection of lava from Eldfell, Iceland, in 1973

Rocks that are formed by volcanic activity can be divided into two groups: pyroclastic rocks, and acid and basic lavas. Pyroclastic rocks are formed from either solid rock fragments or bombs of lava blown out of the throat of a volcano. The bombs solidify as they fly through the air. Rocks formed from hardened lavas vary according to the type of lava. Acid lavas are thick and sticky, flow very slowly, and form steep-sided volcanoes. The more fluid, basic lavas form flatter volcanoes or may well up through cracks in the sea floor. Basic lavas are fast-flowing and so quickly spread out to cover vast areas.

Pyroclastic rocks

Pyroclastic means "fire-broken," an apt name for rocks that consist of rock and lava pieces that were blown apart by exploding gases.

Agglomerate formed close to a vent

JUMBLED PIECES
The force of an explosion may cause rocks to fragment. As a result, a mixture of angular pieces often [blocks?] the central vent or is laid down close to vents. The fragments form rocks known as agglomerates.

VOLCANIC BOMBS
When blobs of lava are thrown out of a volcano, some solidify in the air, landing on the ground as hard "bombs." Bombs can be round or irregular. These two specimens are shaped like footballs.

Intrusion breccia formed within a vent

Ash

INSIDE A VOLCANO
Magma flows through a central vent or escapes through side vents. Underground it may form dikes that cut across rock layers, and sills of hardened magma parallel to rock layers.

Vent

Side vent

Magma

Sill

Dike

Bedded tuff (a hardened ash)

WIND-BLOWN PARTICLES
Tiny fragments of volcanic ash can travel for thousands of miles in the atmosphere. Where it settles and hardens it forms tuff. This ash erupted from Mount St. Helens, Washington, in 1980. The coarse grains were blown three miles (five km) from the crater; the fine particles were carried by the wind for 17 miles (27 km).

Eruption of Mount St. Helens, 19[80]

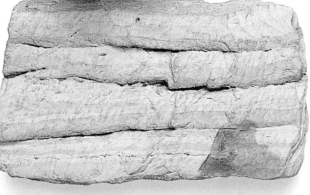

Acid lavas

Thick, sticky acid lavas move slowly and may harden in the volcano's vent, thereby trapping gases. As pressure builds up, the gases may explode to form pyroclastic rocks.

UPTION OF VESUVIUS
e famous eruption in A.D. 79
oduced a *nuée ardente*, a fast-
oving cloud filled with magma and
h. The Roman town of Pompeii
is destroyed in this event.

Aphthitalite

hthitalite

CKS FROM GASES
ctive volcanoes are said to be
rmant." Even when volcanoes
dormant or dying, volcanic
es may escape and hot springs
n. These colorful rocks were
ned in this way at Vesuvius.

FLOATING ROCKS
Pumice is hardened lava froth. Because the froth contains bubbles of gas, the rock is peppered with holes, like a honeycomb. Pumice is the only rock that floats in water. This sample is from the Lipari Islands, Italy.

NATURAL GLASS
Although chemically the same as pumice, obsidian (p. 16) has a totally different glassy texture. Because of its sharp edges, early people used it for tools, arrowheads, and ornaments (p. 29).

CARAMEL-LIKE LAVAS
This light-colored, fine-grained rock is called rhyolite. The distinctive bands formed as the thick, sticky lava flowed for short distances.

Basic lavas

These lavas flow smoothly, and may cover vast distances with a thin layer. As a result, the vent does not get choked and gases can escape, so that although there is plenty of lava, few pyroclastic rocks are formed.

RUNNY LAVAS
Basaltic lavas are fast-flowing and spread out quickly to cover vast areas. This specimen of basalt (p. 17) was deposited by the Hualalai Volcano, one of the many volcanoes on Hawaii.

STRUCTION OF AKROTIRI
s town on Santorini, Greece, was
ied by volcanic ash, c. 1450 B.C.

WRINKLED ROCKS
When lava flows, the surface cools and forms a skin, which wrinkles as the fluid center keeps on flowing. The resulting rocks are called ropy lavas.

MULTI-COLORED BASALT
Sparkling points in this basalt include green olivine and black pyroxene crystals.

Sedimentary rocks

WHEN ROCKS are weathered and eroded (p. 12) they break down into smaller pieces of rock and minerals. This material, which is called sediment, may eventually be carried to a new site, often in the sea or in river beds. The sediments are deposited in layers which become buried and compacted (pressed down). In time the particles are cemented together to form new rocks, known as sedimentary rocks. In large outcrops it is often possible to see the various layers of sediment with the naked eye.

THIN SECTION OF LIMESTONE
Under the microscope (p. 42), fine details in this ammonite limestone are revealed. The ammonite shells (p. 38) show up clearly against the mud background. Ammonites are now extinct, and we know this rock must be about 160 million years old.

Ammonite shell

Mud backgrou

RAW INGREDIENTS *above*
Foraminifera are marine organisms that discharge lime. Although rarely bigger than a pinhead, they play an extremely important part in rock building. When they die the shells fall to the ocean floor, where they eventually become cemented into limestone.

Shell remains embedded in rock

Chalk

Oolitic limeston

Shelly limestone

Gastropod limestone

Remains of gastropod shell

Rounded grains known as ooliths

FLINT
A form of silica (p. 42), lumps of flint are often found in limestones, especially chalk. They are gray or black, but the outside may be covered in a white powder-like material. Like obsidian (p. 16), when flint is broken, it has a "conchoidal" fracture (p. 48).

LIMESTONES
Many sedimentary rocks consist of the remains of once-living organisms. In some, such as these shelly and gastropod limestones, the remains of animals are clearly visible in the rock. However, chalk, which is also a limestone, is formed from the skeletons of tiny sea animals that are too small to see with the naked eye. Another limestone, oolite, forms in the sea as calcite builds up around grains of sand. As the grains are rolled backward and forward by waves, they become larger.

ALGAL LIMESTONE
So-called "muddy" limestones like this are often referred to as landscape marbles. This is because when the minerals crystallize they may produce patterns in the shape of trees and bushes.

...le-filled, ...egular-shaped rock

CALCAREOUS TUFA
This extraordinary looking porous rock is formed by the evaporation of spring water and is sometimes found in limestone caves (p. 22).

EVAPORITES
Some sedimentary rocks are formed from the evaporation of saline waters. Examples of these include gypsum and halite. Halite is also known as rock salt, from which we get table salt. Gypsum is used to make plaster of Paris, and in its massive form is called alabaster. Both halite and gypsum are minerals that can be found in large deposits worldwide at sites where evaporation of sea water has occurred.

Gypsum crystals growing from a central point like daisy petals

Single crystals of rock salt are not found as often as massive samples

Halite

Gypsum

Reddish cast caused by impurities in the salt

GRAND CANYON
...s spectacular scenery was ...ned by the erosion ...d sandstone and ...stone.

Grit

Red sandstone

SANDSTONES
Although both these rocks are made by the cementing together of grains of sand, their texture varies. The red sandstone was formed in a desert, where the quartz grains were rounded and polished by the wind. The grains in grit are more angular, as they were buried quickly, before they could be smoothed by rubbing.

CLAY
Formed of very fine grains that cannot be seen by the naked eye, clay feels sticky when wet. It may be gray, black, white, or yellowish. When it is compacted and all the water forced out of it, it forms hard rocks called mudstone or shale.

...DED VOLCANIC ASH
...many sedimentary rocks it is possible to see ...individual layers of sediments because they ...n visible bands. Here, the stripes are layers ...volcanic ash. The surface has been polished ...highlight this feature.

Flint pebble

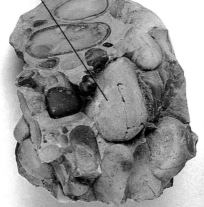

CONGLOMERATE
The flint pebbles in this rock were rounded by water as they were rolled about at the bottom of rivers or seas. After they were buried, they gradually became cemented together to form a rock known as conglomerate.

Large rock fragment

BRECCIA
Like conglomerate, breccias contain fragments of rock. However, these are much more angular because they have not been rounded by water or carried far from their original home - often the scree (broken rocks) at the bottom of cliffs.

Limestone caves

SPECTACULAR CAVES lined with dripping stalactites and giant stalagmites are perhaps the best known of limestone wonders. The caves are formed when rainwater, a weak acid, dissolves calcium carbonate (calcite or lime) out of limestone, a sedimentary rock (p. 20). In addition to caves, this process also produces several other characteristic features including limestone pavements and special landscapes.

Top section attached to roof of cave

Point of intersection

Stalactites of this thickness may take hundreds of years to form

STALACTITES
Stalactites are formed in caves by groundwater containing dissolved lime. The water drips from the roof and leaves a thin deposit as it evaporates. Growing down from the roof, stalactites increase by a fraction of an inch each year and may eventually be many yards long. Where the water supply is seasonal, stalactites may show annual growth rings like those of tree trunks.

Single stalactite formed from two smaller ones growing together

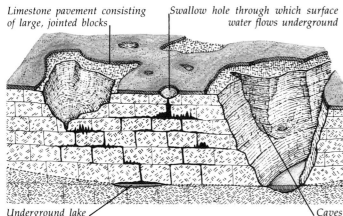

Limestone pavement consisting of large, jointed blocks

Swallow hole through which surface water flows underground

Underground lake

Caves

LIMESTONE LANDSCAPES *above*
Rainwater dissolves calcite in limestone, producing deep, narrow structures ("grikes"). In time, the water dripping down such cracks enlarges them into passages. Although the surface remains dry, flowing water dissolves the rock and produces "swallow holes" at the junctions between grikes. Underground streams flow through caves and form subterranean lakes. Some calcite is redeposited in the caves to form stalactites and stalagmites.

PLAN DE SALES, FRANCE
Limestone pavements consist of large, cracked, flat blocks ("clints") of rock. They occur where weathering of pure limestone leaves nothing behind, such as clay, to make soil.

TUFA
Known as a precipitate, tufa (p. 21) forms when lime is deposited from water onto a rock surface in areas of low rainfall. If a man-made object is left in lime-rich waters it may become coated in tufa.

Coral-like structure

EASE GILL CAVES, ENGLAND
The fine stalactites and stalagmites in this cave form the most spectacular part of a much larger, complex cave system under the hills of the Lancashire Pennines. In fact, this is the largest cave system in Great Britain.

Odd-shaped
stalactite

*Prominent growth
rings mark the gradual
development of the
stalactite as each
deposit formed*

*Point onto which
overhead drips fall*

Orange twin
stalactite

Last section to grow

STONE FOREST, CHINA

The staggering landscape of the Hunan Province of China is typical of karst scenery. Named after the limestone area of Karst in Yugoslavia, the term is applied to many limestone regions, including the Cumberland Plateau, U.S.A., parts of the Blue Mountains, Australia, and the Causses, France.

PAMUKKALE FALLS, TURKEY

Beautiful travertine terraces are formed from the precipitation (separation) of calcite from hot springs in limestone areas. Travertine is quarried as a decorative building stone (p. 27).

STALAGMITES

Stalagmites are formed on the floor of caves where water has dripped from the roof or a stalactite above. Like stalactites, they develop as water containing dissolved lime evaporates. Stalactites and stalagmites can grow together and meet to form pillars. These have been described as "organ pipes," "hanging curtains," and "portcullises."

*Color caused by
impurities in the deposit*

Layer of relatively pure calcite

INSIDE A STALACTITE

This specimen has been sliced through the center to reveal colored bands. The different colors show how the stalactite formed from deposits of lime with varying degrees of purity. The purest parts are the whitest.

*End attached to
floor of the cave*

Metamorphic rocks

Schist

THESE ROCKS get their name from the Greek words *meta* and *morphe*, meaning "change of form," and are igneous (p. 16) or sedimentary (p. 20) rocks that have been altered by heat or pressure or both. Such conditions can exist during mountain-building processes (p. 6); buried rocks may then be subjected to high temperatures and may be squeezed or folded, causing minerals in the rocks to recrystallize and new minerals to form. Other metamorphic rocks are formed when rocks surrounding a hot igneous mass are "baked" by the heat.

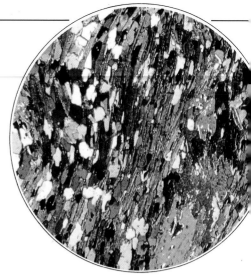

THIN SECTION OF GARNET-MICA SCHIST
Seen through a petrological microscope (p. 42) this Norwegian rock reveals brightly colored, blade-shaped mica crystals. Quartz and feldspar appear as various shades of gray; garnet appears black.

Saccharoidal marble

MARBLES
When limestone is exposed to very high temperatures, new crystals of calcite grow and form the compact rock known as marble. It is sometimes confused with quartzite, which looks similar. However, marble is softer and may easily be scratched with a knife. Some medium-grained marble looks sugary and is called saccharoidal. This specimen comes from Korea. The other two marbles are formed from limestone containing impurites, such as pyroxene.

Knobby gray marble

Impure marble

Evenly sized grains give a sugary appearance

Chiastolite slate

Spotted hornfels

Long chiastolite crystals

Aggregates of carbon

Spotted slate

FROM SLATE TO HORNFELS
The irregular speckles in spotted slate are small groups of carbon crystals formed by heat from an igneous intrusion. In rocks nearer the intrusion, the temperature is much higher and needle-like crystals of chiastolite form in the slate. The rocks very close to the intrusion become so hot that they completely recrystallize and form a tough new rock called hornfels.

Garnet-muscovite-chlorite schist

Blue, bladelike crystals of kyanite

Red garnet crystals

19th-century slate quarry

Kyanite-staurolite schist

SCHISTS

An important group of metamorphic rocks is termed schist. These medium-grained rocks formed from shale or mud but at a higher temperature than slate. For example, the garnet-muscovite-chlorite schist shown here must have been exposed to temperatures of at least 932°F (500°C) because garnet crystals do not grow at lower temperatures. Kyanite-staurolite schist forms under high pressure, 6-9 miles (10-15 km) below the Earth's surface.

LATE

uring mountain building, ale was squeezed so ard that the flaky ineral mica recrystal-zed at right angles to e pressure. The resulting ck, slate, splits easily to thin sheets.

Light-colored layer containing quartz and feldspar

Dark band of biotite

Black biotite crystals

Blue kyanite crystals

Banded gneiss

Crystals of a green variety of pyroxene

ed garnet ystals

Biotite-kyanite gneiss

ECLOGITE

A rock produced under very high pressure, eclogite is extremely dense and is thought to form in the mantle (p. 6) - considerably deeper than most other rocks. It contains pyroxene and small red crystals of garnet.

GNEISSES

At high temperatures and pressures, igneous or sedimentary rocks may be changed to gneisses. They have coarser grains than schists and are easy to identify because the minerals often separate into bands. These layers may be irregular where the rock has been folded under pressure.

Dark host rock

Pink granitic rock

MIGMATITE

Under intense heat parts of rocks may start to melt and flow, creating swirling patterns. This is very often shown in migmatites. They are not composed of one rock but a mixture of a dark host rock with lighter colored granitic rock. This sample is from the Scottish Highlands.

Marble

STRICTLY SPEAKING, marble is a metamorphosed limestone (p. 24). However, the term "marble" is often used in the stone industry for a variety of other rocks. All are valued for their attractive range of textures and colors, and because they are easily cut and polished. Marble has been widely used for sculpture, particularly by the ancient Greeks; its use in building reached a peak under the Romans.

IN THE RAW *below*
A true marble, this unpolished, coarse crystalline specimen of Mijas marble is from Malaga, Spain. Looking at uncut rock, it is hard to imagine the pattern a polished sample will reveal.

MEDICI MADONNA
Michelangelo sculpted this statue from Carrara marble, c. 1530.

CARRARA QUARRY
The world's most famous marble comes from the Carrara quarry in Tuscany, Italy. Michelangelo used it, since it was the local stone.

ITALIAN SPECIALTY *left*
Gray Bardilla marble comes from Carrara, Italy, an area famous for its marble production.

GREEK CONNECTION
Originally from the Greek island of Euboea, streaked Cipollino marble is now quarried in Switzerland, the island of Elba, and Vermont. It was used in the Byzantine church of Saint Sophia in Istanbul, Turkey.

ITALIAN ELEGANCE *right*
Another striking Italian marble is the black and gold variety from Liguria.

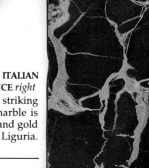

TUSCAN STONES
The distinctive texture of
the Italian decorative stone
breccia violetto was the reason for
its use in the Paris Opera House in 1875.

J MAHAL
lia's most famous monument is
de of assorted marbles.

**SOUTH
AFRICAN SWIRLS**
Polished travertine, a
variety of tufa (p. 21
and p. 23), has beautiful
swirling patterns. This
specimen is from Cape
Province, South Africa.

SWISS ORIGINS
The limestone breccia
known as macchia-
vecchia is quarried in
Mendrisio, Switzerland.

Detail of marble
inlaywork on the
Taj Mahal

AFRICAN COPPER *left*
The vivid coloring of
green verdite is caused
by the presence of
copper. It comes
from Swaziland,
Africa.

ALGERIAN ROCK *bottom*
Breche Sanguine or Red African
is a red breccia (p. 21) from
Algeria. The Romans used
it in the Pantheon, Rome.

The first flint tools

Bᴇᴄᴀᴜsᴇ ꜰʟɪɴᴛ sᴘʟɪᴛs in any direction, fractures to a sharp edge, and is fairly widespread, it was adopted by prehistoric people to fashion sharp tools. In the beginning these were crude choppers, but gradually more complex weaponry and tools such as scrapers and knives were developed.

Rough flint chunk found in Chalk areas

*Leather thong securing fl[...]
and antler sleeve to han[...]*

TOOLS FROM FLINT
Flint was shaped by chipping flakes from a chunk to leave a core that gradually became more refined.

Sharp edged tool use[...]
for skinning and cutt[...]

STONE ON STONE
The earliest tools were made by striking a stone against the flint to remove chips and leave sharp jagged edges.

PRESSURE FLAKING
Better cutting edges and finer chips were made with sharp, pointed objects, such as antler bone.

Scrapers were used to dress animal hides during the Neolithic period (4000-2300 B.C.)

Flint flakes and chippings

Cutting e[...]

Large sharpened hand axe

Light-colored hand axe

Small sharpened hand axe

Crude early chopper

Rough cutting edge

Ear[...]
men usi[...]
hand ax[...]

HAND AXES
Stone Age hand axes were used for smashing animal bones, skinning hunted animals, cutting wood, and sometimes even for cutting plants. The well-developed, dark axes are 300,000-70,000 years old. The smaller of the two may once have been larger and been reduced by sharpening. The lighter-colored axe dates from around 70,000-35,000 B.C.

Sharp cutting edge

Hafted adzes were used to hollow out and shape canoes

solithic adze

Antler sleeve

HAFTED ADZES

Adzes had uneven (asymmetrical) cutting edges, and the blade was at a right angle to the handle, or haft. They were used for shaping wood, and were swung from above rather than the side. These specimens date from the Mesolithic period (10,000-4000 B.C.).

Adze mounted directly onto handle

Asymmetrical cutting edge of flint

DANISH AXE AND DAGGER

This Early Bronze Age axe, found in the river Thames in England, is known to be an imported piece because of its shape. This fact and the careful polish applied to it suggest it would have been a valuable object. This is also true of the Early Bronze Age flint dagger (2300-1200 B.C.). Its shape imitates the earliest copper daggers, which would have been very rare, highly valued items at first.

Axe

Flint dagger

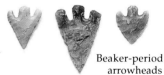

ARROWHEADS

Although the bow and arrow was first invented in the preceding Mesolithic period, it continued to be used for hunting in the Early Neolithic period, when leaf-shaped arrowheads were common. Later, in the Beaker period (2750-1800 B.C.), barbed arrowheads became characteristic. It was a time of change with the introduction of metalworking.

Neolithic leaf-shaped arrowheads

Beaker-period arrowheads

SICKLE

Flint sickles indicate the growing of crops. The long, slightly curved blade was used for harvesting. Sometimes the sickles have a "gloss" on their cutting edge, which is a polish caused by repeated harvesting. This one, mounted in a reproduction handle, is of Neolithic age (4000-2300 B.C.).

Reproduction wooden handle

Reproduction wooden handle

FLINT DAGGERS

These two daggers are also from the Beaker period. Their rarity, and the care with which they were made, suggest they may have served as both status symbols and weapons.

9th-century obsidian axe from Mexico

Spearhead with obsidian blade from the Admiralty Islands, off Papua New Guinea

OBSIDIAN

Like flint, obsidian was fashioned into early tools because it fractures with sharp edges. It was also used as a primitive mirror.

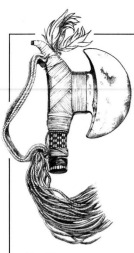

Rocks as tools

Flint was not the only rock used by early people. Archaeologists have found numerous examples of stone implements from many different cultures around the world. Some were used as weapons, others as agricultural or domestic tools, ranging from mortars (for grinding) to storage vessels and make up palettes. Many weapons appear never to have been used, and may have been purely status symbols.

Brazilian stone axe

Neolithic axe showing a highly polished surface

Neolithic axe made of diorite, an igneous rock

Neolithic axe made of rhyolitic tuff, a volcanic rock

STONE AXES

All these stone axes date from the Neolithic period in Britain (4000-2300 B.C.). They are highly polished and tougher than flaked flint axes. They must have been traded over long distances, as the source rocks were hundreds of miles from the places where the axes were found.

Wedge to keep the stone from moving

Bored quartzite pebble

WEIGHTED DIGGING ST

Pebbles, like this quart example, were someti pierced and used to weight the of pointed wooden sticks. Du the Mesolithic and Neolithic peri (10,000-2300 B.C.) such sticks were u to break up the ground to p crops or grub up ro

Breaking ground wi digging s prior to plant

Reproduction wooden stick

Sharpened wooden point for digging hard ground

BATTLE-AXES

These perforated axes (pierced with holes) belong to the Early Bronze Age (2300-1200 B.C.). The top two could have served as weapons but the bottom one is usually described as an axe-hammer because one end could have been used as an axe, the other as a hammer. Because they are preserved so well they were probably for display as much as for use.

Side view of battle-axe made of diori

Top view of battle-axe

Dual-purpose granite axe-hammer

Hammer en

Axe end

Carved stone maul - a war club or mace - made by Haida Indians, a North American tribe who live on islands off British Colun bia, Canada

South African digging stick with horn point and stone weight

WHETSTONES

Bronze implements were sharpened by rubbing the blunt edge against a long whetstone. Often the stones were perforated so that they could be hung on loop around the neck or belt. These whetstones re from the Bronze Age (2300-700 B.C.).

Engraved Viking forge stone made of soapstone, used in making metal weapons and tools

A bird-shaped mortar carved by Haida Indians (opposite)

MARBLE MAKE UP PALETTE

Roman cosmetics included chalk and powdered lead to whiten the face and arms, red ochre to tint the lips and cheeks, and soot to darken the eyebrows. Using fine bronze or bone spoonlike objects, small amounts were placed on stone palettes and mixed with water or a water-soluble gum. They could then be applied as a paint or paste.

STONE SPINDLE WHORL *right*

The Romans also used stones as spindle whorls. The end of wool or cotton fibers was attached to a bone or wooden spindle weighted with the whorl. As the spindle hung down, its weight and rotating motion helped the twisting of the thread, which was then wound onto the spindle.

Handle

Rotating stone

OMAN ROTARY QUERN

uring Roman times a portable quern (mill) as used for grinding corn in the home. It nsisted of two stones: the lower one was dded in earth or fixed to a bench, and the pper stone, held in position by a spindle, as rotated above it by means of the ndle. The grain was fed through e hole in the upper stone; the tary motion forced it between e grinding surfaces.

Jsing a stone quern to grind corn during the Iron Age

Conglomerate stone (p. 21) attached to a bench or bedded in the earth

ain dy for nding

Pigments

WHEN EARLY PEOPLE started to paint their homes and bodies, they did not have to look far for pigments to color paints and dyes. By crushing local colored rocks and mixing the powders with animal fats, they produced a range of colors. As trading routes expanded over the centuries, new colors were introduced. Many of the pigments were toxic (poisonous), so their colors are now produced in the laboratory.

Brown clay

Powder
brown cl

EARTHY HU
Clays were used a l
by early artists becau
they were widely availat
and, being fine-grained, we
easy to grind up. They pr
duced mostly drab gre
and brown colo

Green clay

Powdered
green clay

Ocher paint

Umber paint

SHADES OF WHITE
The earliest white pigment was chalk (p. 20), although in some areas kaolin (china clay) was used instead.

Powdered chalk

CAVE PAINTI
The earliest known artworks we
done by cavemen using a mixt
of clays, chalk, earths, and bu
wood and bon

COLOR VARIATION IN A MINERAL
Many minerals are always the same color. This is useful for identifying them. Some, however, exhibit a range of colors. For example, tourmaline (p. 55) may occur as black, brown, pink, green, and blue crystals or show a variety of colors in a single crystal.

Chalk white paint

Bison from Grotte de Niaux, France, c. 20,000 B.C.

COLOR CLUES
A useful aid in identification is the color produced when a mineral is finely crushed. The simplest way to do this is to scrape the sample gently across an unglazed white tile. Many minerals leave a distinct colored streak that may or may not be the same color as the mineral; others crush to a white powder and leave no visible mark.

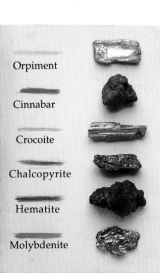

Orpiment

Cinnabar

Crocoite

Chalcopyrite

Hematite

Molybdenite

Powdered charco

BLACK AS COAL
Still popular with artists today, charcoal was well known to cave painters. They found plentiful supplies in the embers of their fires.

Lamp black paint

Powdered
hematite

Powdered realgar

Arsenic
orange
paint

N COLORING
earthy variety of
atite produces a rich
dish-brown pigment. Very
ly powdered material was also used
skin make up and has been employed
fine polishing medium (jewelers' rouge).

Red paint

EGYPTIAN ORANGE
About 1500 B.C.
Egyptians first crushed
realgar, an arsenic compound
found in hot-spring deposits, to
form an orange pigment.
Medieval artists preferred
to use the mineral cinnabar.

Powdered
malachite

Powdered
orpiment

Malachite
green
paint

King's yellow
paint

FOOL'S GOLD
Medieval artists
used orpiment, an
arsenic compound, to
make many colors and
to imitate gold. Its resem-
blance to gold made some
chemists of the time try to
extract the noble metal from it!

LLIANT GREEN
achite, a copper compound,
duces a rich bright green. It
first used during the Bronze Age in Egypt.

Powdered
lapis lazuli

Ultramarine
paint

Powdered
azurite

Powdered
cinnabar

PRECIOUS BLUE
The refinement of
lapis lazuli (p. 52)
powder into rich ultra-
marine blue was first
achieved in Persia.
Because it was expensive, it
was used less often than azurite.

NATURAL VERMILION
The bright vermilion
red of cinnabar
(mercuric sulfide)
was used in
China in
prehistoric
times, but
only came into
widespread use
in the Middle Ages
(5th-15th centuries).
Vermilion was later
made from mercury
and sulfur.

BRIGHT PAINTING
By the late 13th century
artists were regularly
using ultramarine
and vermilion,
as in this
painting
by Duccio.

SSICAL BLUE
rite, a
er com-
nd, was one of
great blue
nents of early
ples. This sample is
icularly earthy and
ld have produced a fine,
ly prized pigment.

Azurite
blue paint

Vermilion
paint

Building stones

Quarrying in the early 19th century was still done almost entirely by manual labor

Mᴏsᴛ ᴏꜰ ᴛʜᴇ ɢʀᴇᴀᴛ ᴍᴏɴᴜᴍᴇɴᴛs of the past - the pyramids, temples, and palaces - have survived because they were made from tough, natural stone. Good building stones must be relatively easy to work but cannot crumble, split, or weather too easily. Today, natural building stones, such as marbles (p. 26), are used mainly as decorative stones, and man-made materials are used for construction.

NUMMULITIC LIMESTONE
This piece of nummulitic limestone was quarried near Cairo, Egypt. It contains small nummulite fossils and was formed about 40 million years ago. The Pyramids were built with stone from the same quarries.

The Pyramids, Egypt, made of local limestone

Fossils

Tooling

PORTLAND STONE
The surface marks on this English limestone are produced by "tooling," a decorative technique that was popular in the last century. After the Great Fire of London in 1666, Portland stone was used to rebuild St. Paul's Cathedral.

OOLITIC LIMESTO
Some 160 million years old, this lim stone is used as a building stone and sometimes in the m facture of cement.

Welsh slate

MOSAIC FLOOR
Small fragments of local stones were often used to make detailed mosaic floors.

160-million-year-old limestone used for roofing

SLATE
Unlike most building materials, roofing stones must split easily into thin sheets. Slate (p. 25) is ideal. However, where it was not available, builders used local, often inferior, stone for roofing.

NOTRE DAME, PARIS
The famous Parisian cathedral was built of local limestone from the St. Jacques region of Paris between 1163 and 1250. The Paris catacombs (underground tombs) are old quarries.

Interlocking roof tile

Pantile

SANDSTONES
Various colored sandstones make excellent building stones. The French town of Carcassonne is built mostly of sandstone, as are many fine old monuments in India.

Man-made stones

People are now able to manufacture building stone substitutes such as brick and tiles, cement, concrete, and glass. However, all these products originate from rocks of some kind.

ROOFING TILES
In many parts of the world, man-made roofing tiles are molded and fired from clay.

Textured buff brick

230-million-year-old sandstone

RANITE
requently used to cover large uildings, polished granite is so used for gravestones. Much f Leningrad, Russia, including e imperial palaces, is made f imported Finnish granite.

EMPIRE STATE BUILDING, NEW YORK
Although mostly made of granite and sandstone, it contains some man-made materials as well.

Smooth red brick

Red sandstone from Scotland used as a cladding building stone

GREAT WALL OF CHINA
The 4,000-mile (6,400-km) long Great Wall, the largest single structure on Earth, is built of various materials depending on the terrain it passes through. Sections include brick, granite and various local rocks.

BRICKS
Easily molded clays are fired to make bricks. Impurities in clays produce bricks of different colors and strengths, making them good for a number of uses.

CEMENT
Cement is made by grinding and heating a suitable limestone. When mixed with sand, gravel, and water, it produces concrete, perhaps the most common building material today.

The story of coal

THE COAL we burn today is millions of years old. It started off as vegetation in the swampy forests that covered parts of Europe, Asia, and North America. As leaves, seeds, and dead branches fell to the wet forest floor, they began to rot. This soft, rotting material later became buried. The weight of the layers above gradually squeezed the water out and compressed the plant material into a solid mass of peat and eventually coal. As pressure and heat increased, five different types of coal were formed, one after the other.

Plant roots

FOSSILIZED WOOD
Jet is a hard black material obtained from driftwood fragments laid down in the sea. It is very light. Often polished, carved, and made into jewelry or decorative objects, jet has been used since the Bronze Age.

"COAL" AS JEWELRY
A major source of jet is found in Yorkshire, northern England. These Roman pendants were found in York and so were almost certainly made of local material.

OIL SHALE
This sedimentary rock is called oil shale because oil can be removed from it. It contains an organic substance of plant and animal origin called kerogen. When heated, this gives off a vapor that contains oil.

Leaf

Stalk

d case

THE ORIGINS OF COAL

Carboniferous (coal-forming) swamps of 270-350 million years ago may have looked like this stylized engraving.

THE RAW INGREDIENTS OF COAL

For coal to form, there must be thick layers of vegetation in areas with poor drainage, such as swamps or bogs. The dead plants become water-logged, and although they start to rot, they cannot decay completely.

THE PEAT LAYER

Peat is a more compact form of the surface layer of rotting vegetation. Some plant roots and seed cases are still visible. In certain parts of the world, where new peat is form-ing today, it is cut and dried, then burned as a fuel.

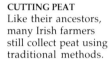

CUTTING PEAT

Like their ancestors, many Irish farmers still collect peat using traditional methods.

BROWN COAL

When peat is compressed, it forms a crumbly brown substance called lignite which still contains recognizable plant remains. Ninety percent of undried peat is water; lignite contains only 50 percent water.

COAL SEAMS

Layers of coal are called seams. They are sandwiched between layers of other material, such as sandstones and mudstones, which were formed by deposits from rivers. These lignite seams are in a French quarry.

"BLACK GOLD"

Under pressure, lignite is changed into bituminous or household coal. It is hard and brittle and has a very high carbon content. It is dirty to handle because it contains a charcoal-like, powdery substance. A lump of coal may have alternating shiny and dull layers and recognizable plant material, such as spores.

CONDITIONS IN THE MINES

During the Industrial Revolution in England, many children were forced to work extremely long hours in horrible conditions in under-ground mines, as this 1842 engraving shows.

MINING FOR COAL

People have been mining coal since the Middle Ages. At "strip" mines, all the coal is removed from the surface. Most other mines are several hundred yards beneath the land or sea, and a lot of mechanized equip-ment is used.

THE HARDEST COAL

The highest-quality coal is called anthracite. This shiny substance is harder than other coal and clean to touch. It is the most valuable of all the coals because it contains the most carbon and produces the most heat and the least smoke.

Fossils

A FOSSIL is a rock containing the preserved remains of once-living animals or plants. Fossils are formed when an animal or plant is buried in sediment. Usually the soft parts rot away, but the hardest parts remain. This is why most fossils consist of the bones or shells of animals, or the leaves or woody parts of plants. In some marine fossils, shells may be replaced by other minerals, or an impression of the insides or outsides may be preserved. Fossils are found in sedimentary rocks, especially limestones and shales. Many fossils are of plants and animals now extinct, such as dinosaurs. They reveal details about the animals and plants that existed millions of years ago, and enable scientists to date the rocks in which they appear. Fossils showing footprints or burrows rather than remains are called trace fossils.

Muddy rock

Impression of leaf

Beech leaf

LEAF IMPRINT
This preserved leaf similar to the mode beech leaf. Even the it is about 40 millio years old, much of t original detail and texture can still be s

Magnolia leaf fr Miocene per

Neuropteris - a seed fern - fossilized in ironstone

PLANT FOSSILS
Many fernlike fossils are found in coal-bearing rocks (p. 36). Formed in the Carboniferous period, they are called Coal Measures fossils. Although they are not exactly the same species as the ferns that grow today, many are very similar.

Fern from the Carboniferous period

Present-day fern

Fronds of a fern called *Asterotheca* preserved in stone

Section of a
nautilus shell

NAUTILUS

Like the ammonite's,
the shell is divided into
chambers. By regulating the
gas in these chambers, the
animal moves up or down in the water. It swims
backward with its head pointing down.

ANCIENT ANCESTORS

This limestone is about 200 million years old.
It is packed with the remains of hundreds of
ammonites. These sea creatures, now extinct,
had hard, coiled shells. Because the species
changed rapidly and lived in many areas of the
world, they can be used to determine the ages of
the rocks in which they occur. The nearest
modern relative of the ammonite is nautilus,
which lives in the Pacific Ocean.

Ammonite remains

A GRAVEYARD FOR SNAILS

This piece of limestone contains the hard spiral
shells of marine gastropods (snails) from
about 120 million years ago. In places,
the white shell has dissolved, leav-
ing an impression of the inside.

Impression of interior of shell

Gastropod shell

FOSSIL HUNTING

The abundance of
fossils at the seashore
made collecting a
popular pastime
during the 19th
century.

Garden snails

Rocks from space

Every year about 19,000 meteorites, each weighing over 4 oz (100 g), fall to the Earth. Most fall into the sea or on deserts, and only about five are recovered annually. Meteorites are natural objects that survive their fall from space. When they enter the Earth's atmosphere their surfaces melt and are swept away, but the interiors stay cold. As meteorites are slowed down by the atmosphere, the molten surface hardens to form a dark, thin "fusion" crust.

PASAMONTE FIREBALL
Photographed by a ranch foreman in New Mexico at 5 A.M., this fireball fell to Earth in March 1933. Meteorites are named after the places where they fall, this one being Pasamonte. The fireball had a low angled path about 500 miles (800 km) long. It broke up in the atmosphere and landed as dozens of meteoritic stones.

Gray interior consisting mainly of the minerals olivine and pyroxene

Fragme
of meteor

Dark, glas
fusion cr
formed duri
passage throu
Earth's atmosph

METALLIC METEORITE
The Cañon Diablo (Arizona) meteorite collided with the Earth about 20,000 years ago. Unlike Barwell, it is an iron meteorite. These are rarer than stony meteorites and consist of an iron-nickel alloy containing about 5-12 percent nickel. They once formed parts of small asteroids (opposite) which broke up. The largest meteorite known is the Hoba (Namibia, Africa) which is iron and weighs about 60 tons. This cut piece of Cañon Diablo has been polished and partly etched with acid to reveal its internal structure.

EARTH'S CONTEMPORARY *above*
The Barwell meteorite fell at Barw
Leicestershire, England, on Christm
Eve, 1965. The meteorite is 4.6 billic
years old and formed at the same
time as the Earth but in a different
part of the solar system. Of every
ten meteorites seen to fall, eight are
stones like Barwell.

METAL AND STONE *bel*
"Stony-irons" form a separate gro
of meteorites. The surface of t
slice of the Thiel Mountains meteo
has been cut and polished to sh
bright metal enclosing stony mater
the mineral olivine. It w
found in Antarctica where meteori
have been on Earth for about 300,0
years and for much of this ti
have been encased in i

EXPLOSION CRATER
When the Cañon Diablo meteorite hit Arizona, about 15,000 tons of meteorite exploded. It created an enormous hole, Meteor Crater, about 0.75 mile (1.2 km) across and nearly 600 ft (180 m) deep. Only 30 tons of meteorite remained, scattered as small fragments across the surrounding countryside.

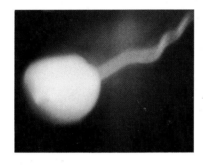

Metal

Stony part containing oliv

HALLEY'S COMET
Water-bearing meteorites may have come from comets, such as Halley's - here depicted in the Bayeux tapestry, which tells the story of the Norman Conquest of England in 1066.

ASTEROID STRUCTURE
Many meteorites come from minor planets, or asteroids. They were never part of a single planet, but circle around the sun between the orbits of Mars and Jupiter. The largest aster-oid, Ceres, is 632 miles (1,020 km) across. Most asteroids are less than 62 miles (100 km) in diameter. Their interiors consist of a central core of metal, which is the source for some iron meteorites like Cañon Diablo; a core-mantle region which provides stony-iron meteorites like Thiel Mountains; and a crust which provides stony meteorites like Barwell.

ust
antle
ore-antle
re

WATER BEARERS
The Murchison meteorite fell in Australia in 1969. It contains carbon compounds and water from space. Material similar to this is believed to form the nucleus of a comet. The carbon compounds were formed by chemical reactions and not by a living organism. Such meteorites are rare - only about three falls in 100 are of this type.

Rocks from the Moon and Mars

Ive meteorites found in Antarctica are known to have come om the Moon because they are like lunar highlands rocks ollected by the Apollo missions. Eight other meteorites e thought to have come from Mars.

MARTIAN ORIGIN
The Nakhla stone fell in Egypt in 1911 and is reported to have killed a dog. This stone formed 1,300 million years ago, much more recently than most meteorites, and probably came from Mars.

LUNAR DISCOVERIES
The lunar meteorites are made of the same material as the lunar highlands boulder next to Apollo 17 astronaut Jack Schmitt.

MOON ROCK
The Moon's surface is covered with soil made of tiny rock and mineral fragments. It was formed by repeated bombardment of the surface by meteorites. Material like this on the surface of an asteroid was compressed to form many stony meteorites. Here, the light-colored mineral is feldspar, and the darker mineral is pyroxene.

Rock-forming minerals

Petrological microscope

COMPOSITION OF TH[E] EARTH'S CRUST
In weight per cent order, the elements ar[e] oxygen (1), silicon (2), aluminum (3), iron (4), calcium (5), sodium (6), potassium (7), magnesium (8), and all other elements (9).

Eight elements make up nearly 99 percent of the Earth's crust. These elements combine to form naturally occurring minerals. Silicate minerals and silica form in most common rocks except limestones. Igneous rocks form the greatest part of the rocky interior of the earth, and specific rock-forming mineral groups are characteristic of certain types of igneous rocks.

Minerals in granitic rocks

The minerals that form granitic and dioritic rocks include feldspars, quartz, micas, and amphiboles. Feldspars are the most abundant of all minerals and occur in nearly all types of rock.

Group of black prismatic crystals with calcite

Single hornblende crystal

SILICA MINERALS
These include quartz, chalcedony (p. 52), and opal (p. 5[?] Quartz is one of the most widely distributed minerals found in igneous, sedimentary, and metamorphic rocks. It is characteristic of granites, gneisses, and quartzites.

Quartz or rock crystal

POTASSIC FELDSPARS
Orthoclase is found in many igneous and metamorphic rocks. Microcline (the lower-temperature form of orthoclase) is found in granite pegmatites.

Green microcline (or amazonstone) crystal

Twinned crystals of pink orthoclase

Hornblende, an amphibole, common in igneous rocks and in metamorphic rocks such as hornblende schists

Tremolite, an amphibole, common in metamorphic rocks

THIN SECTION OF A GRANITIC ROCK
When a slice of diorite about 0.03 mm thick is viewed under a petrological microscope (above), it reveals colored amphiboles, plain gray to colorless quartz, and lined gray plagioclase feldspar.

Biotite, a dark, iron-rich mica usually found in igneous rocks, is also common in schists and gneisses

Silvery, radiating, needle-like crystals

AMPHIBOLES
This group of minerals is widely found in igneous and metamorphic rocks. Amphiboles can be told apart from pyroxenes (opposite) by the characteristic angles between their cleavage planes (p. 48).

Muscovite, an aluminum-rich mica, is abundant in schists and gneisses

Silvery brown tabular crystals

MICAS
There are two main types of mica: dark iron- and magnesium-rich mica, and white aluminum-rich mica. All have perfect cleavage (p. 48) and split into thin flakes.

Minerals in basic rocks

The seven minerals shown here are all commonly found in basic rocks like basalts and gabbros.

Pink anorthite crystals, a plagioclase feldspar, with augite

Twinned albite crystals, a plagioclase feldspar, with calcite

OLIVINE

This silicate of iron and magnesium is typically found in silica-poor rocks such as basalts, gabbros, and peridotites. It often forms as small grains or large, grainy masses. Clear crystals are cut as gem peridots (p. 54).

— Green olivine crystals

Volcanic bomb containing olivine, from Vesuvius (p. 18)

Single crystal of augite

Nepheline, a feldspathoid, with calcite

PLAGIOCLASE FELDSPARS *above*

This series of minerals contains varying amounts of sodium and calcium. Plagioclase feldspars are common in igneous rocks.

FELDSPATHOIDS

As their name suggests, these minerals are related to feldspars, but they contain less silica and are typically formed in silica-poor volcanic lavas.

THIN SECTION OF A BASIC ROCK

A section of olivine basalt in polarized light reveals brightly colored olivine, brown-yellow pyroxene, and minute lined, gray plagioclase feldspars.

Leucite crystal, a feldspathoid, on volcanic rock

Prism-like crystal of enstatite with biotite

Greenish-black prism-like crystals of augite, a pyroxene

PYROXENES

The most common pyroxenes are calcium, magnesium, and iron silicates. Augite is a common pyroxene and is found abundantly in igneous rocks such as gabbros and basalts. Less common is enstatite, which is found in gabbros, pyroxenites, and some peridotites.

Other rock-forming minerals

There are two other important groups of rock-forming minerals - carbonates and clays.

CARBONATES

These are important constituents of sedimentary (limestones) or metamorphic (marble) rocks, also in ore vein deposits. The most common is calcite, the main ingredient of limestones.

Dolomite, a carbonate, found in some sedimentary deposits usually interlayered with limestones

Montmorillonite

Illite

Kaolinite (china clay) formed from partly decomposed orthoclase

CLAYS

An important part of the sedimentary rock sequence, clays form from the weathering and alteration of aluminous silicates. Clays include kaolinite, montmorillonite, and illite.

Crystals

THROUGH THE AGES people have been fascinated by the incredible beauty of crystals. For centuries it was thought that rock crystal, a variety of quartz, was ice that had frozen so hard it would never thaw. The word "crystal" is derived from the Greek word *kryos,* meaning "icy cold." In fact, a crystal is a solid with a regular internal structure. Because of the arrangement of its atoms, a crystal may form smooth external surfaces called faces. Different crystals of the same mineral may develop the same faces but they may not necessarily be the same size or shape. Many crystals have important commercial uses, and some are cut as gemstones (p. 50).

Crystal collecting in the Alps, c. 1870

Light reflecting on the crystal face

Crystals orientated in different directions

Lines of striations formed as the crystal grew

Large twin crystal

Plane of intersection

Well-developed faces

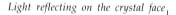

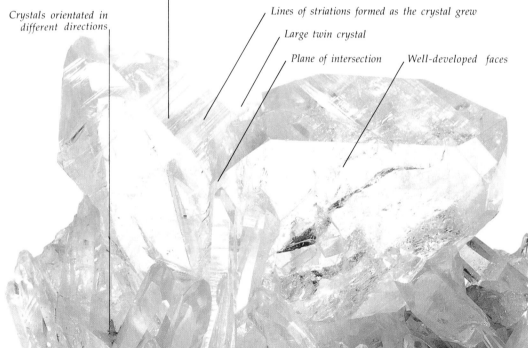

SCULPTED "ICE"
Beautiful groups of natural crystals like this rock crystal look as if they have been artificially cut and polished. This specimen, found in Isère, France, is particularly well-formed consisting of a large twin crystal (opposite) and many simple crystals. The narrow ridges and furrows across some of its faces are called striations. These were formed when two different crystal faces attempted to develop at the same time.

Crystal symmetry

Crystals can be grouped into the seven systems shown below according to their symmetry. This is reflected in certain regular features of the crystal. For example, for every face there may be another on the opposite side of the crystal that is parallel to it and similar in shape and size. However, it may be hard to see the symmetry in many mineral specimens because crystals occur in groups and do not have well-developed faces.

SCIENTIFIC MEASUREMENT
A useful feature in identifying crystals is that the angle between corresponding faces of a particular mineral is always the same. Scientists measure this accurately using a contact goniometer.

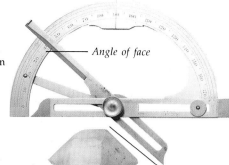

Angle of face

Angle between crystal faces being measured

TRICLINIC
Crystals in this system have the least symmetry - as shown by this wedge-shaped axinite crystal from Brazil. Plagioclase feldspars (p. 43) are also triclinic minerals.

CUBIC
Metallic pyrite (p. 59) forms cube-shaped crystals but other cubic mineral forms include octahedra (with eight faces) and tetrahedra (four faces). Garnet (p. 55) is also classified in this system. Crystals in this system have the highest symmetry.

TETRAGONAL
Dark green idocrase crystals, like this Siberian specimen, are grouped with zircon (p. 54) and wulfenite (p. 9) in the tetragonal system.

ORTHORHOMBIC
Common ortho-rhombic minerals include baryte (from which we get barium for medicinal uses), olivine (p. 43), and topaz (p. 54).

RHOMBOHEDRAL (TRIGONAL) *below*
Smaller secondary crystals have grown on this siderite crystal. Quartz (opposite), corrundum (p. 51), tourmaline (p. 55), and calcite (pp. 22 and 48) belong to the same system.

MONOCLINIC
The most common crystal system includes gypsum (from which we make plaster of Paris; p. 21), azurite (p. 33), and orthoclase (p. 49).

HEXAGONAL *above*
Beryl (p. 50), including this Colombian emerald variety, crystallizes in the hexagonal system as does apatite (p. 49) and ice. (But each snowflake is different from every other.)

Snowflakes

Twinning

Crystals may grow in groups in cavities in mineral veins. Occasionally they develop in such a way that two (or sometimes more) individual crystals appear to intersect in a symmetrical manner. Related crystals like this are known as twin crystals.

CONTACT TWINS
The crystal form of the mineral cerussite is orthorhombic. This group of twin crystals is from Southwest Africa.

PENETRATION TWINS
Staurolite is also an orthorhombic mineral. In this cross-shaped Brazilian specimen one twin appears to penetrate into the other.

Twinned gypsum crystals form a distinctive arrow shape from which they get their common name, "swallow-tail"

The growing crystal

No two crystals are exactly alike because the conditions in which they develop vary. They can only grow where there is sufficient space, and if this is restricted, distortions or unusual features may develop. Crystals range in size from microscopic to several yards long. The shape and size of a crystal or aggregate (mass) of crystals is called its habit.

Coral-like sh

WHITE CORAL
Aragonite, which was named after the Spanish province of Aragon, can sometime have a "coralloid" habit. This term is used describe minerals whose shape resembles corals.

Fine crystal "needles"

RADIATING NEEDLES
Long, slender, crystals with a needle-like appearance are described as having an "acicular" habit. In this scolecite specimen, gray acicular crystals radiate from the center.

METALLIC "GRAPES"
Some chalcopyrite (p. 59) crysta grow outward from a center and such aggregates appear as rounde knobs. The habit is "botryoidal," a term strictly meaning like a bunch of grapes.

SPARKLING AGGREGATE *below right*
Hematite (p. 33) occurs in a number of different habits. When it forms shiny, sparkling crystals it is said to have a "specular" habit, named from the Latin *speculum*, meaning "to reflect."
The specimen shown consists of an aggregate of specular crystals.

CRYSTAL COLUMNS
"Prismatic" crystals are much longer in one direction than in other two. This beryl crystal (p. 50) has six large rectangular prism faces and a flat hexagonal terminal face at each end.

Equant garnet crys

Mica sc

SOFT STRANDS *left*
Crystals of tremolite, one of several minerals commonly known as asbestos, are soft and extremely bendable. Their habit is known as "fibrous" because the crystals resemble material fibers.

LAYERED SHEETS
Certain minerals, including mica (p. 42), divide into thin sheets (p. 48). They are said to be "micaceous" or, alternatively, "foliated" (meaning leaflike) or "lamellar" (meaning thin and platelike).

EQUAL S
Many minerals develop crystals tha almost equal in all dimensions, and then said to be "equant." This specim garnet (p. 55) in mica schist is a fine exam

rite (p. 59)

UAL FORM

rite (p. 59) may crystallize as simple cubes
d also as 12-faced solids called pentagonal
odecahedra. If the conditions change during
owth, both forms may develop at the same time,
sulting in striations (p. 44) on the crystal faces.

*trongly
triated
ubic faces*

*Sloping
dodecahedral faces*

*Top of glistening pink
calcite crystal group*

*Base of
gray calcite
crystal group*

PARALLEL LINES

During crystal growth a series of crystals of the same
type may develop and grow in the same direction. This
calcite aggregate shows a number of tapering pale
pink and gray crystals parallel to each other.

SALT LAKE, CYPRUS
When salt lakes dry up, a thick
crust of soluble salts is left.

Stepped faces

STEPPED CRYSTALS

This specimen of halite (p. 21) contains
numerous sand grains. It shows
more growth in two direc-
tions, resulting in a
stack of cubic crystals
forming steps.

DOUBLE DECKER

Chalcopyrite (p. 59)
and sphalerite (p. 57)
crystals have similar
structures. Here,
tarnished, brassy
metallic chalcopyrite
crystals have grown
in parallels on
brownish-black
sphalerite crystals.

Sphalerite crystals

*Chalcopyrite
crystals*

Sandy cubes

HOPPER GROWTH

The mineral halite (salt, p. 21) is
cubic, but crystals sometimes grow
from solution faster along the cube
edge than in the center of the faces.
This results in "hopper crystals"
that have stepped cavities in
each face.

ANCHING METAL

here space is restricted, like in the confined spaces
tween two beds of rock, native copper (p. 56)
d other minerals may grow in thin
eets. Its characteristic branchlike
rm is described as "dendritic."

*Branches"
copper*

*Outline
of chlorite*

PHANTOM GROWTH

The dark areas within this quartz
crystal formed when a thin layer
of chlorite coated the crystal at an
earlier stage of its growth. As the
crystal continued to grow, the chlorite
became a ghostlike outline.

The properties of minerals

THE MAJORITY OF MINERALS have a regular crystal structure and a definite chemical composition. These determine the physical and chemical properties that are characteristic for each mineral, some having a great deal of scientific and industrial value. By studying mineral properties such as cleavage, hardness, and specific gravity, geologists can discover how the mineral was formed and use them, along with color and habit (p. 46), to identify minerals.

Structure

Some chemically identical minerals exist in more than one structural state. The element carbon, for example, forms two minerals - diamond and graphite. The difference in their properties is caused by different arrangements of carbon atoms.

Carbon atom

Model of graphite structure

GRAPHITE
In graphite, a hexagonal mineral formed under high temperature, each carbon atom is closely linked to three others in the same plane. The structure is made of widely spaced layers that are only weakly bonded together. Graphite is one of the softest minerals (Mohs' scale 1-2), and its loose bonding enables it to leave marks on paper, which is why it is used in pencils.

Graphite specimen

Model of diamond structure   *Carbon atom*

Model showing how one atom is bonded to four others

Diamonds

DIAMOND
In diamond (p. 50), a cubic mineral formed under high pressure, each carbon atom is strongly bonded to four others to form a tight, rigid structure. This makes diamond extremely hard (Mohs' scale 10). Because of this, it is used as a cutting tool in industr

Cleavage

When crystals break, some tend to split along well-defined cleavage planes. These are caused by the orderly arrangement of the atoms in the crystal.

Thin layers

THIN SHEETS
Stibnite, an ore of antimony, shows a perfect sheet-like cleavage because of weak bonds between antimony and sulfur atoms.

LEAD STEPS
Galena, the main ore of lead (p. 57), has a perfect cubic cleavage, because of the internal arrangement of lead and sulfur atoms. A broken crystal face consists of many small cubic cleavage steps.

Steps

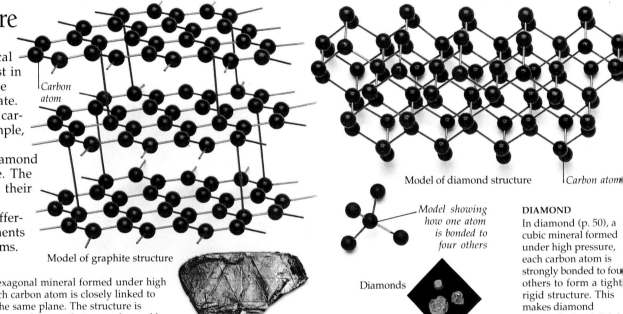

PERFECT BREAK
Baryte crystals (p. 45) show an intersecting, perfect cleavage. If this crystal was broken, it would split along these planes of cleavage.

Thin lines show cleavage planes

Smaller crystal growing with larger crystal

PERFECT RHOMB
Any piece of calcite has such a well-developed rhombohedral cleavage that a break in any other direction is virtually impossible.

FRACTURE
Quartz crystals break with a glassy, conchoidal (shell-like) fracture rather than cleaving along any particular plane.

Rounded, conchoidal edges

Hardness

The bonds holding atoms together determine a mineral's hardness. In 1812, the Austrian mineralogist Friedrich Mohs devised a scale of hardness that is still in use today. He selected ten minerals as standards and arranged them so that any mineral on the scale would scratch only those below it. Everyday objects can be used to test where a mineral fits into the scale. A fingernail has a hardness of 2.5, and a penknife is 5.5. Minerals of six and above will scratch glass; glass will scratch apatite and other minerals below it.

GRAPH SHOWING RELATIVE HARDNESS
The intervals between the minerals in Mohs' scale are irregular. Diamond is about 40 times harder than talc, and corundum is only nine times as hard.

1	2	3	4	5	6	7	8	9	10
Talc	Gypsum	Calcite	Fluorite	Apatite	Orthoclase	Quartz	Topaz	Corundum	Diamond

Magnetism

Only two common minerals, magnetite and pyrrhotite (both iron compounds), are strongly magnetic. Some specimens of magnetite called "lodestones" were used as an early form of compass.

NATURAL MAGNET
Magnetite is permanently magnetized and will attract iron filings and other metallic objects such as paper clips.

Clusters of iron filings

Optical properties

As light passes through minerals, many optical effects are produced due to the way light reacts with atoms in the structure.

DOUBLE IMAGE
Light traveling through a calcite rhomb is split into two rays, making a single daisy stalk appear to the eye as two.

FLUORESCING AUTUNITE
When viewed under ultraviolet light, certain minerals fluoresce (give off light).

Specific gravity

This property relates a mineral's chemical composition to its crystal structure. It is defined as the ratio of the weight of a substance to that of an equal volume of water. Determining the specific gravity may aid identification.

SIZE vs. WEIGHT
The nature of the atoms and the way they are arranged in a mineral determines its specific gravity. These three mineral specimens all weigh the same, but because the atoms in quartz and galena are heavier or more closely packed together than those in mica, the quartz and galena specimens are much smaller.

Mica

Quartz

Galena

Gemstones

GEMSTONES are minerals that occur in nature and are valued for their beauty and rarity, and because they are hardy enough to survive everyday wear on jewelry and other objects. Diamond, emerald, ruby, sapphire, and opal all fit this description. Light reflects and refracts (changes direction) with the minerals to produce the intense colors of ruby and emerald and the "fire" of diamond. Color, fire, and luster (shine) are usually revealed only by skilled cutting and polishing (p. 60). Gems are commonly weighed by the carat, equal to one fifth of a gram, and not to be confused with the carat used to describe the quality of gold (p. 59).

Beryl

The most important gem varieties - emerald and aquamarine - have been used for centuries: Egyptian emerald mines date back to 1650 B.C. Beautifully formed hexagonal beryl crystals may be found in pegmatites and schists in Brazil, Russia, and many other countries.

Cut emerald

EMERALDS
The finest emeralds, such as those in the British Crown Jewels, come from Colombia, South America, where they occur in veins with calcite and pyrite. Flawless emeralds are very rare; most crystals are fractured or contain other minerals. These may seem to detract from a stone, but in fact they may be crucial in proving its natural origin.

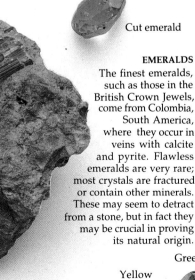

THE ASSORTED COLORS OF BERYL
Pure beryl is colorless. The gems' colors are due to impurities such as manganese which produces the pink of morganites. Greenish-blue aquamarine crystals are often heat-treated to produce a more intense blue color.

Yellow heliodor

Greenish heliodor

Pink morganite

ROMAN BERYL JEWELRY
The earrings and necklaces contain cut emeralds.

Aquamarine

Diamond

Diamond is named from the Greek word *adamas*, meaning "unconquerable," and is the hardest of all known minerals (p. 49). It is famed for its lasting fiery brilliance. The quality of a gem diamond is measured by its color, its clarity, the quality of its cut, and its carat weight popularly known as "the four C's."

Kimberley mine, South Africa

Diamond crystal
Kimberlite

TREASURES IN GRAVEL
Before 1870 diamonds were found only as crystals fragments in river gravels, mainly in India or Bra In the late 1800s the discovery first of diamond-bearing gravel and th kimberlite ma South Africa t leading suppli

DIAMONDS IN ROCK
Kimberlite is the source rock for most diamonds. It is named after Kimberley in South Africa, where it occurs in a volcanic pipe that has its roots between 100 and 200 miles deep in the Earth's crust.

MULTI-COLORED DIAMONDS
Diamond ranges from colorless through yellow and brown to pink, green, and blue. Red diamond is very rare. To show off the stones to their best advantage, for centuries diamond cutters have fashioned table and rose-cut stones (p. 60) and, more recently, "brilliant" cuts which display the gem's fire and luster.

KOHINOOR DIAMOND
This famous Indian diamond, here worn by Queen Mary of England, was presented to Queen Victoria in 1850.

Corundum

The beauty of ruby and sapphire lies in the richness and intensity of their colors. Both are varieties of the mineral corundum, which is colorless when pure. Tiny quantities of chromium give rise to the red of ruby, and iron and titanium are responsible for the blues, yellows, and greens of sapphire.

SAPPHIRE CRYSTAL
While ruby tends to form in flat crystals, sapphires are generally shaped like barrels or pyramids. They often feature zones of blue to yellow color that are important in choosing which crystals to cut.

RIVER JEWELS
Most sapphires and rubies are taken from gem-rich gravel. The gem minerals are usually harder and more resistant to chemical weathering than their parent rocks and become concentrated in river beds.

STAR SAPPHIRE
Some stones contain very fine needle-like crystals orientated in three directions. Proper cutting will give star rubies or star sapphires.

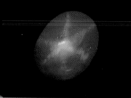

RUBY CRYSTAL
Known as the Edwardes Ruby, this crystal is of exceptional quality, weighing 162 carats. It is almost certainly from the famous gem deposits of Mogok, Burma.

Cut ruby

GEMSTONES IN JEWELRY
The oldest jewelry comes from ceremonial burials 20,000 years ago. Here, rubies, emeralds, and diamonds decorate a late 16th-century enameled gold pendant.

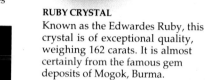

Blue sapphire

Pink sapphire

Clear sapphire

Colorless sapphire

Mauve sapphire

Yellow sapphire

GEM SOURCES
Australia is the most abundant source of blue and yellow sapphires; rubies are mined in Burma, Thailand, and central Africa. The rich gem gravel of Sri Lanka has for at least 2,000 years supplied exceptional blue and pink sapphires.

Opal

The name opal probably derives from the Sanskrit word *upala*, meaning "precious stone". However, the opals used by the Romans in their jewelry did not come from India, but from Czechoslovakia. In the 16th century, opal was brought to Europe from Central America and only after 1870 did Australia become the main supplier.

OPAL MINING IN AUSTRALIA
Aside from its use in jewelry, opal mined today is also used in the manufacture of abrasives and insulation products.

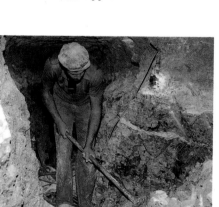

COLOR VARIATIONS IN OPAL
The beautiful blue, green, yellow, and red rainbow in precious opal is caused by the reflection and scattering of light from tiny silica spheres inside the mineral. This is different from the background or "body" color, which may be clear as in water opal, milky as in white opal, or gray, or black as in the most precious form, black opal.

Black opals

Milky opal

White opal

OPAL'S ROCKY ORIGINS
Most opal forms over long periods of time in sedimentary rocks, as in this sample from Australia. However, in Mexico and Czechoslovakia opal forms in gas cavities in volcanic rocks. It is often cut as cabochons (p. 60). The opal veins in sedimentary rocks are usually thin, and slices of these may be glued onto onyx or glass to form "doublets." These stones are sometimes made even more valuable by adding a cap of clear quartz to form a "triplet."

FIRE OPAL
The finest fire opal comes from Mexico and Turkey and is generally cut as faceted stones. It is valued for the intensity and rainbow quality of its colors.

Decorative stones

Turquoise, agate, lapis lazuli, and jade are all gems made up of many crystals. They are valued mainly for their color, either evenly distributed as in fine turquoise, or patterned as in an agate cameo. The toughness of jade and agate makes them ideal for delicate carving, and the softer turquoise is used for "protected" settings, such as pendants or inlay. Lapis lazuli is variable in quality and fine carving is only possible in high-quality material.

Chalcedony

Carnelian, onyx, agate and chrysoprase are all forms of chalcedony. Pure chalcedony is translucent (frosty) gray or white and consists of thin layers of tiny quartz fibers. Obviously banded chalcedony is called agate. Impurities cause the different colors and patterns.

Chrysoprase cabochon

ANCIENT FAVORITE
Apple-green chrysoprase has been used in jewelry since pre-Roman times, often as cameos or intaglios (p. 61) in rings and pendants.

Vein of turquoise

Turquoise

Found in the earliest jewelry, turquoise is so universally recognized that "turquoise blue" is an accepted term for a pale greenish blue. Its color is largely due to copper and traces of iron. The more iron that is present, the greener (and less valuable) the turquoise.

TURQUOISE ORNAMENTS
This object may be from ancient Iran (Persia). The double-headed serpent (top) is an Aztec necklace. It was sent to Cortez by Montezuma during the early 16th century.

CUT TURQUOISE
The finest sky-blue turquoise occurs in Nishapur, Iran, where it has been mined for about 3,000 years. Another ancient source, known to the Aztecs, is the southwestern United States. Today this area supplies most of the world's turquoise.

Lapis lazuli

Blue lapis lazuli is composed mainly of the minerals lazurite and sodalite with smaller amounts of white calcite and specks of brassy colored pyrite.

ANCIENT LAPIS JEWELRY
For centuries lapis has been fashioned into beads and carvings. It has been known for over 6,000 years and is named from the Persian word *lazhward*, meaning "blue."

PUREST SAMPLES
The best lapis lazuli is mined in Badakhshan, Afghanistan, where it occurs in veins in white marble.

ANCIENT ARABIC MOSAIC
Lapis was used to decorate the wooden box known as the Standard of Ur, c. 2500 B.C.

EGYPTIAN AMULET
Many fine pieces of early Egyptian craftsmanship have been recovered from the tombs of the kings.

TRUE BLUE *left*
The vivid blue of this lapis slice is caused by small amounts of sulfur, and has been imitated in glass and synthetic lapis.

AGATE
Fine-grained, banded agates form in cavities in volcanic rocks. The most abundant sources of good agate are in Brazil and Uruguay.

POLISHED AGATE
The beautiful patterns shown in polished agate slices were caused by hot, silica-rich solutions filtered through rocks. The crystals then formed in bands and colored deposits.

CARVED PORTRAIT
Bloodstone cameos were popular in Roman times.

Crystals

Deep-colored band

STONE LANDSCAPE
The pattern in moss agate or mocha stone is well shown in this delicate cabochon.

ORNAMENTAL KNIFE
Carnelian is red chalcedony and has been used widely in decorative jewelry and inlay work throughout history. Here it has been fashioned into a knife.

Jade
Originally named from the Spanish *piedra de hijada*, used to describe the green stone carved by the Indians in Central America, jade actually refers to two different substances - jadeite and nephrite.

MOGUL DAGGER
Pale green and gray nephrite was a favorite material of the Mogul (Indian) craftsmen, who fashioned dagger handles, bowls, and jewelry, often inlaid with rubies and other gems.

RARE JADE
Jadeite may be white, orange, brown, or, rarely, lilac, but the most prized is "imperial jade," a translucent emerald-green variety.

CHINESE ART
The toughness of jade was known to the Chinese more than 2,000 years ago and they used this to make many delicate carvings. These were done in nephrite until Burmese jadeite became available, c. 1750.

TUTANKHAMEN'S MASK
Lapis, carnelian, obsidian, and quartz are inlaid in gold along with assorted colored glass.

NEPHRITE BOULDERS
Nephrite is more common than jadeite and is generally green, gray, or creamy white. Much jade occurs as waterworn boulders. This example of nephrite from New Zealand is typical.

Lesser-known gems

IN ADDITION TO the well-known gemstones such as diamond, ruby, sapphire, emerald, and opal, many other minerals have been used for human adornment. Beautiful features like the luster and fire of zircon and demantoid garnet, and the multicolored hues of the tourmaline family, have attracted attention. There is space here only to glimpse some examples of the stones more frequently seen in jewelry, but the range of color even in these species is extensive.

Multicolored topaz

Blue topaz

Yellow topaz

TOPAZ
Occuring chiefly in granites and pegmatites, some gem-quality topaz crystals are very large, weighing many pounds. The largest stones are colorless or pale blue. The most valuable in terms of price per carat are golden yellow - "imperial topaz" - or pink, both of which are found in Brazil. Pakistan is the only other source of pink topaz. Yellow topaz is slightly more common, and colorless topaz is found worldwide.

Blue spinel

Pink spinel

Mauve spinel

TOPAZ BROOCH
Brown topaz was commonly used in 18th- and 19th-century jewelry. The rarer pink stones were man-made by heating yellow topaz.

SPINEL
Red spinels are very similar to rubies. They were once called balas rubies, probably after Balascia, now Badakhshan in Afghanistan, their supposed source. Fine red spinels also come from Burma, and from Sri Lanka, where there is also a range of pink, lilac, blue, and bluish-green stones.

Cut spinel

BLACK PRINCE'S RUBY
This famous spinel is the central stone in the British Imperial State Crown.

PERIDO
This is the transparent gem variety of olivin (p. 43), a mineral common in basaltic lavas and som deep-seated igneous rocks. The amount of iron i the mineral determines the shade of color - th more valuable golden-green and deep-green stone contain less iron than those with a brownish tinge Peridot is softer than quartz and has a distinctiv oily luster, and has beeen use in jewelry since Roma times. The original sourc was the island of Zebirge in the Red Sea, but fin material has since com from Burma, Norway, an Arizon

Vermilion zircon

Pink zircon

Green zircon

Yellow zircon

Blue zircon

ZIRCON
Named from the Arabic word *zargoon*, meaning "vermilion" or "golden colored," stones of these colors, in addition to green and brown varieties, have been used in jewelry in India for centuries. When transparent stones are cut and polished they display a luster and fire similar to diamond, but they are softer and chip more easily.

Cut peridots

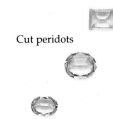

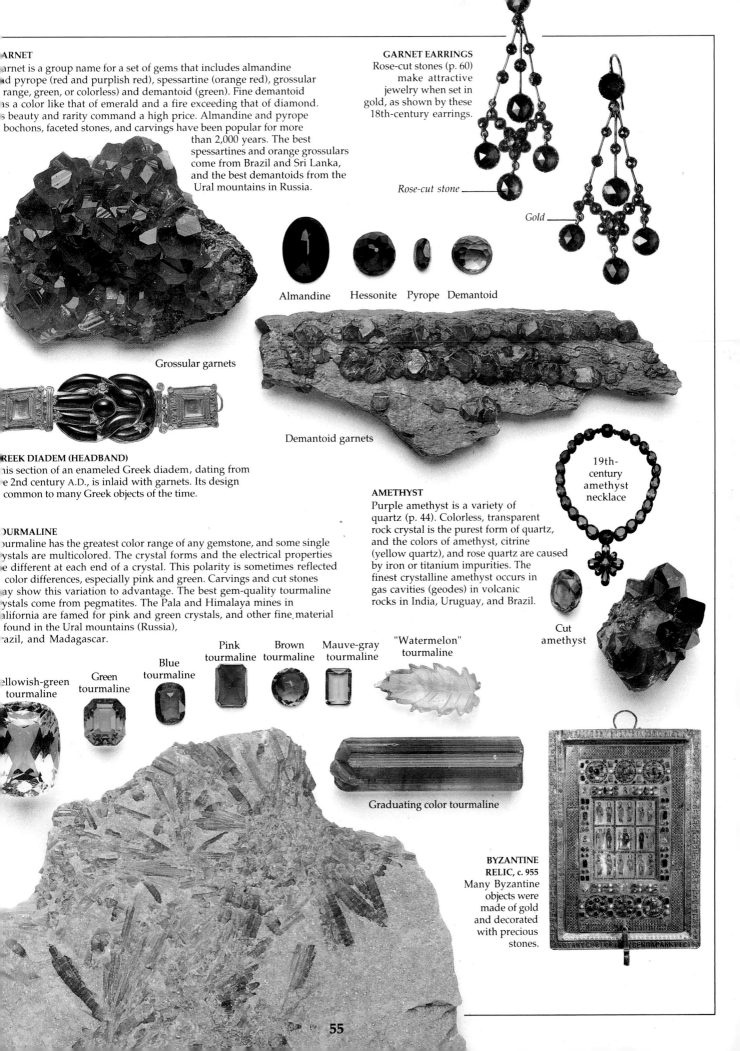

GARNET

Garnet is a group name for a set of gems that includes almandine and pyrope (red and purplish red), spessartine (orange red), grossular (orange, green, or colorless) and demantoid (green). Fine demantoid has a color like that of emerald and a fire exceeding that of diamond. Its beauty and rarity command a high price. Almandine and pyrope cabochons, faceted stones, and carvings have been popular for more than 2,000 years. The best spessartines and orange grossulars come from Brazil and Sri Lanka, and the best demantoids from the Ural mountains in Russia.

GARNET EARRINGS
Rose-cut stones (p. 60) make attractive jewelry when set in gold, as shown by these 18th-century earrings.

Rose-cut stone

Gold

Almandine Hessonite Pyrope Demantoid

Grossular garnets

Demantoid garnets

GREEK DIADEM (HEADBAND)
This section of an enameled Greek diadem, dating from the 2nd century A.D., is inlaid with garnets. Its design is common to many Greek objects of the time.

TOURMALINE
Tourmaline has the greatest color range of any gemstone, and some single crystals are multicolored. The crystal forms and the electrical properties are different at each end of a crystal. This polarity is sometimes reflected in color differences, especially pink and green. Carvings and cut stones may show this variation to advantage. The best gem-quality tourmaline crystals come from pegmatites. The Pala and Himalaya mines in California are famed for pink and green crystals, and other fine material is found in the Ural mountains (Russia), Brazil, and Madagascar.

AMETHYST
Purple amethyst is a variety of quartz (p. 44). Colorless, transparent rock crystal is the purest form of quartz, and the colors of amethyst, citrine (yellow quartz), and rose quartz are caused by iron or titanium impurities. The finest crystalline amethyst occurs in gas cavities (geodes) in volcanic rocks in India, Uruguay, and Brazil.

19th-century amethyst necklace

Cut amethyst

Yellowish-green tourmaline

Green tourmaline

Blue tourmaline

Pink tourmaline

Brown tourmaline

Mauve-gray tourmaline

"Watermelon" tourmaline

Graduating color tourmaline

BYZANTINE RELIC, c. 955
Many Byzantine objects were made of gold and decorated with precious stones.

Ore minerals and metals

Bronze ritual food vessel from
China, c. 10th century BC

ORE MINERALS are the source of most useful metals. After
the ores are mined, quarried, or dredged (from lakes and rivers),
they are crushed and separated, then refined and smelted
(fused and melted) to produce metal. Even before 5000 B.C.,
copper was used to make beads and pins. However, it was the
Mesopotamians (ancient Arabs) who first
began large-scale smelting and casting. Then, around 3000 B.C.,
tin was added to copper to produce bronze, a harder metal.
Still more important was the production of iron, fairly
widespread by 500 B.C. Iron was harder than bronze, and iron
ores were much more common.

Bauxite –
aluminum
ore (p. 13)

Iron mining, c. 158

LIGHTWEIGHT ALUMINUM
Aluminum is a good conductor of
electricity, lightweight, and
not easily corroded. It is used
in power lines, building and
construction, cars
and washing
machines, pots
and pans.

Aluminum kitchen foil

Stacks of
aluminum
ingots

Hematite -
iron ore

Steel screw

TOUGH IRO
Hematite, the most important iron or
commonly occurs as "kidney ore" - s
called because of its shape. Iron is toug
and hard, yet easy to work. It can b
cast, forged, machined, rolled, an
alloyed with other metals. It is use
extensively in the constructio
industries. Steel and mar
household items are mac
from iro

*Chalcopyrite
coppe
o*

Rutile -
titanium ore

STRONG TITANIUM
Rutile and ilmenite are the principal
ores of titanium. Usually found in
igneous or metamorphic
rocks, these two minerals are
concentrated by weathering.
They form deposits with
other minerals, many of which
are removed as by-products.
Because of its light weight and
great strength, titanium is widely
used in aircraft frames and engines.

COLORFUL COPPER
Brassy yellow
chalcopyrite and
bluish-purple bornite
are common copper
ores. Massive ores are
usually found in
isolated deposits that
are too expensive to
mine. Most copper now
comes from large, low-
grade deposits. Because
it is a good conductor,
copper is used in the
electricity industry,
and because it is easy
to shape and roll, it is
good for household
water pipes.
It is used in
alloys with
zinc (brass)
and with tin
(bronze).

*Borni
cop*

Copper
plumbing
joint

Airliner partially
constructed from titanium

DURABLE NICKEL
Nickel comes from deposits in large layered gabbroic intrusions (p. 17) and from deposits formed by the weathering of basaltic igneous rocks. Small amounts of nickeline occur in silver and uranium deposits where nickel is a by-product. Nickel is used in alloys like stainless steel to help it resist corrosion. High-strength, high-temperature alloys are suitable for aircraft and jet engines.

Nickeline - nickel ore

Sphalerite - zinc ore

Nickel alloy battery

LACKJACK ZINC
phalerite or "black-ck," as it was ommonly known by iners, is the most nportant zinc ore and found in deposits in edimentary and olcanic rocks. Its name omes from the Greek ord for "deceptive," s it has sometimes een mistaken for other inerals. Zinc is used ainly in galvanizing," whereby sheet steel is oated with a thin ayer of zinc to prevent from rusting.

Zinc processing in Belgium, c. 1873

Cinnabar - mercury ore

RED MERCURY
The poisonous mercury ore cinnabar (p. 33), is found in only a few locations, those in China, Spain, and Italy being the best known. It forms near volcanic rocks and hot springs. Mercury is very dense, has a low melting point, and is liquid at room temperature. It is widely used in the manufacture of drugs, pigments, insecticides, and scientific instruments, as well as in dentistry.

Mercury thermometer

OFT AND SHINY LEAD
alena, the main lead ore, is orked chiefly from deposits in mestones, such as those in the uthern U.S. Some lead deposits e mined only because of their gh silver content. Lead is the nsest and softest common metal d is very resistant to rrosion, but it is not ry strong. It is used in orage batteries, soline, engineering, d plumbing, and ith tin in solder.

Lead solder

Galena - lead ore

19th-century Cornish tin mine, England

Crystalline cassiterite - tin ore

WORKABLE TIN
The tin ore cassiterite is hard, heavy, and difficult to scratch. Crystalline forms, like this Bolivian specimen, are relatively rare. Tin has a low melting point and does not corrode easily. It is nonpoisonous, easy to shape, and a good conductor of electricity. It is used in solder and tinplate (although aluminum is now more widely used for canning). Pewter is an alloy with roughly 75 percent tin and 25 percent lead.

Tin can

alvanized il

Precious metals

GOLD AND SILVER were among the earliest metals discovered and were valued for their beauty and rarity. Both were used in coins and bars which were visible items of wealth, and were used to buy things. Gold and silver were used on jewelry and other objects. Platinum was first reported from Colombia, South America, in the mid-18th century but was not widely used in jewelry and coins until this century.

Silver

Silver tarnishes (discolors) easily and is less valuable than either gold or platinum. Both sterling and plated silver are made into jewelry and ornaments, and silver is also used in the photographic industry.

MEXICAN ORE CRUSHER
Early methods of crushing silver ore were primitive but effective

Platinum

Currently more valuable even than gold, platinum is used in oil refining and in reducing pollution from car exhausts.

SPERRYLITE CRYSTAL
Platinum is found in a variety of minerals, one of which is sperrylite. This well-formed crystal was found in the Transvaal, South Africa, around 1924. It is the world's largest known crystal of this species.

PLATINUM GRAINS
Most platinum minerals occur as very small grains in nickel deposits. However, platinum-bearing grains are also commonly found in gold workings. These grains are from Rio Pinto, Colombia.

DELICATE SILVER WIRES
Silver is now mostly removed as a by-product from the mining of copper and lead-zinc deposits. In the last century, it was usually mined as native metal (above). Particularly famous are silver "wires" from the Kongsberg mines in Norway.

CELTIC BROOCH
The Celts fashioned many intricate pieces of jewelry in silver.

PLATINUM NUGGET
Very rarely, large nuggets of platinum are found. This one, from Nijni-Tagilsk in the Ural mountains of Russia, weighs 2.4 lb (1.1 kg). The largest ever recorded weighed 21.4 lb (9.7 kg).

RUSSIAN COINS
Platinum has been used for coins in several countries. During the reign of Nicholas I, the Russians minted platinum coins worth three roubles.

SILVER BRANCHES
Occasionally, as in this specimen from Copiapo, Chile, silver occurs in delicate, branchlike "dendritic" forms (p. 47).

RELIGIOUS BELL
One of a pair, this silver Torah bell was made in Italy in the early 18th century and was used in Jewish ceremonies.

old

day this familiar yellow metal is important in jewelry, dentistry, and
ctronics, yet more than half the gold, mined with so much labor, returns to
e earth - buried in bank vaults for investment purposes!

OUTH AFRICAN MINE
Traditional gold mining
methods required much
labor, c. 1900.

THE GREAT GOLD RUSH
During the 19th century, the discovery of
gold in both California and Australia
fired the imagination of thousands
of prospectors who began panning
in earnest.

Crystalline
chalcopyrite

FOOL'S GOLD
Amateurs some-
times mistake
either chalco-
pyrite or pyrite
for gold because of
its brassy color,
hence the term
"fool's gold."
Chalcopyrite, the
main ore of copper,
is greenish yellow
compared to gold,
and is more brittle
and harder,
although not as
hard as pyrite.

Massive
chalcopyrite

IN GOLD
ld may occur in
artz veins and
metimes forms rich
crustations. The gold is
moved by crushing the ore
d obtaining a concentrate,
ich is then smelted.

PYRITE
Pyrite generally forms cubic crystals and, on a fresh surface, is
closer in color to "white gold" or electrum, an alloy of gold and silver,
than to pure gold. However, pyrite is much harder than gold.

GOLD GRAINS
Gold is also produced
from the rounded
grains that occur in
some gravel and sand
deposits. These
deposits are worked
either by panning or
larger-scale
dredging. The gold
particles are removed
before smelting.

nkhamen's collar

Crystalline
pyrite

Massive pyrite

EGYPTIAN CRAFT
The ancient Egyptians
were one of the earliest
civilizations to master the
art of goldsmithing. They
used solid, beaten gold.
Nowadays, copper and
silver are often added to
make the gold harder.
The gold content is then
measured in carats.

Cutting and polishing stones

T HE EARLIEST METHOD of fashioning stones was to rub one against another to produce a smooth surface that could then be engraved. Much later, professional craftsmen (lapidaries) became skilled at cutting precious stones to obtain the best optical effect and to maximize the size of the cut stone. In recent years, amateur lapidaries have shaped rounded "pebbles" of various minerals by going back to the process of rubbing stones together, using a rotating drum.

Grinding and polishi agates in a Germ workshop, c. 18

Cutting gems

When mined, many gem-stones look dull (p. 50). To produce a sparkling gem, the lapidary must cut and polish the stone to bring out its natural beauty, bearing in mind the position of any flaws.

THE HARDEST CUT
Rough diamonds are marked with India ink before cutting.

POPULAR CUTS
The first gemstones were cut into relatively simple shapes, such as the table cut, and cabochon cut. Later lapidaries experimented with more complex faceted cuts, such as the step cut for colored stones, and the brilliant for dia-mond and other colorless stones.

Table cut

Cabochon

Rose cut

Emerald or step cut

Pear brilliant

Round brilliant

Hollow drum

Belt driven by motor

Lid of dru

Rollers

TUMBLING
A tumbling machin an electrically driv hollow drum mount on rollers. Mineral fragments are tumbl in the drum with co grit and water for a a week. This is re-peated with finer g until the pebbles ar rounded and polish

TUMBLING ACTION
As the drum rotates, pebbles are smoothe and rounded by the and by each other.

Water add with gr

Rough mineral pieces ready for tumbling

GRITS AND POLISHES
Various grinding grits are used in sequence from the coarsest to the finest, followed by a polishing powder.

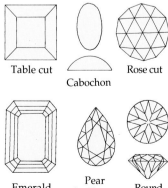

Coarse grinding grit used in first tumbling

Fine grinding grit used for second tumbling

Cerium oxide, very fine polish powder, used finally to make pebbles smooth and sparkling

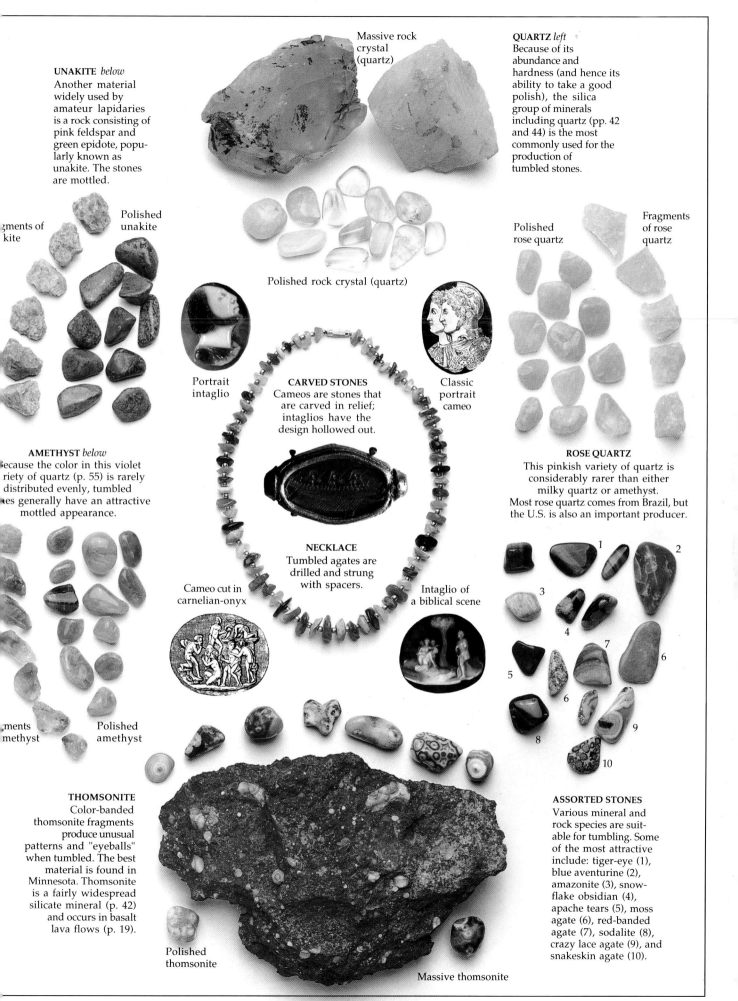

UNAKITE *below*
Another material widely used by amateur lapidaries is a rock consisting of pink feldspar and green epidote, popularly known as unakite. The stones are mottled.

gments of kite

Polished unakite

Massive rock crystal (quartz)

QUARTZ *left*
Because of its abundance and hardness (and hence its ability to take a good polish), the silica group of minerals including quartz (pp. 42 and 44) is the most commonly used for the production of tumbled stones.

Polished rock crystal (quartz)

Polished rose quartz

Fragments of rose quartz

Portrait intaglio

CARVED STONES
Cameos are stones that are carved in relief; intaglios have the design hollowed out.

Classic portrait cameo

AMETHYST *below*
ecause the color in this violet riety of quartz (p. 55) is rarely distributed evenly, tumbled ies generally have an attractive mottled appearance.

NECKLACE
Tumbled agates are drilled and strung with spacers.

ROSE QUARTZ
This pinkish variety of quartz is considerably rarer than either milky quartz or amethyst. Most rose quartz comes from Brazil, but the U.S. is also an important producer.

Cameo cut in carnelian-onyx

Intaglio of a biblical scene

ments methyst

Polished amethyst

THOMSONITE
Color-banded thomsonite fragments produce unusual patterns and "eyeballs" when tumbled. The best material is found in Minnesota. Thomsonite is a fairly widespread silicate mineral (p. 42) and occurs in basalt lava flows (p. 19).

Polished thomsonite

Massive thomsonite

ASSORTED STONES
Various mineral and rock species are suitable for tumbling. Some of the most attractive include: tiger-eye (1), blue aventurine (2), amazonite (3), snowflake obsidian (4), apache tears (5), moss agate (6), red-banded agate (7), sodalite (8), crazy lace agate (9), and snakeskin agate (10).

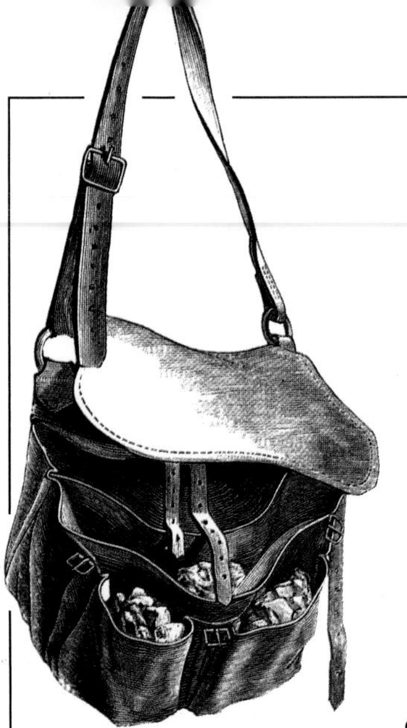

Collecting rocks and minerals

THE COLLECTING OF MINERAL and rock specimens and the recording of finds is a rewarding and popular pastime. As a hobby, it is in a tradition that dates back to the amateur geologists of the 19th century, many of whom had impressive collections.

COLLECTING TOOLS
The basic equipment required is a geological hammer, weighing between 1 and 2 lb (0.5 and 1 kg), and a range of chisels. Geological hammers usually have a square head and a chisel edge used for splitting rocks. They are specially made for the job; other types of hammer should not be used because they are more likely to splinter.

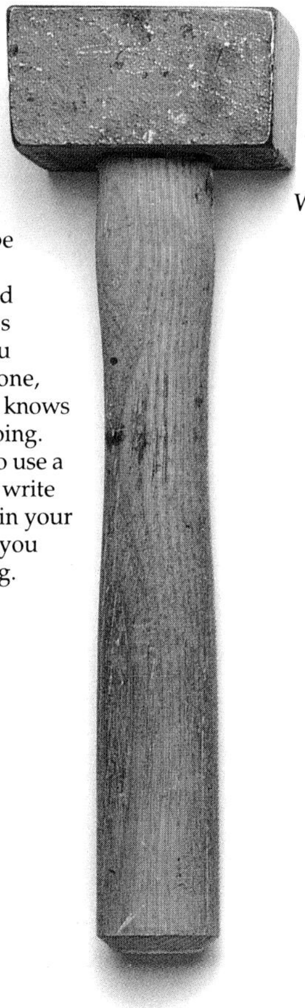

Club hammer for use with chisels

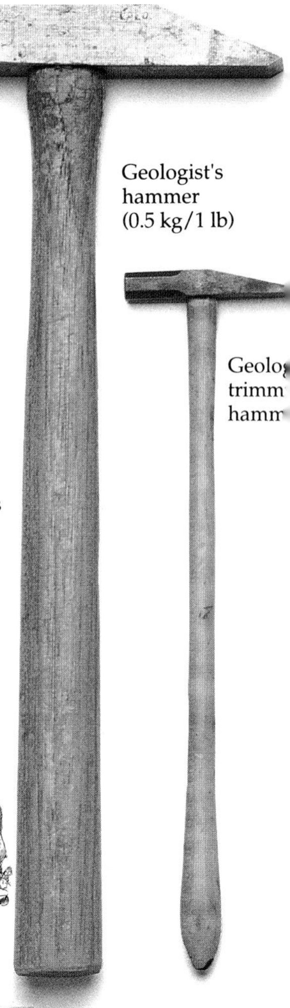

Geologist's hammer (0.5 kg/1 lb)

Geolo trimm hamm

Wide-ended chisel

Sharp pointed chisel

CAREFUL PLANNING
All field work and collecting trips should be planned in advance using geological guide books and maps. Permission must be obtained to visit any area or site on private land. It's a good idea to take a friend along, but if you are collecting alone, make sure someone knows where you are going. If you know how to use a compass, you can write down the bearings in your notes each time you find something.

FIELD WORK
During the 19th century, geologists working in the field developed the techniques of collecting and mapping rocks.

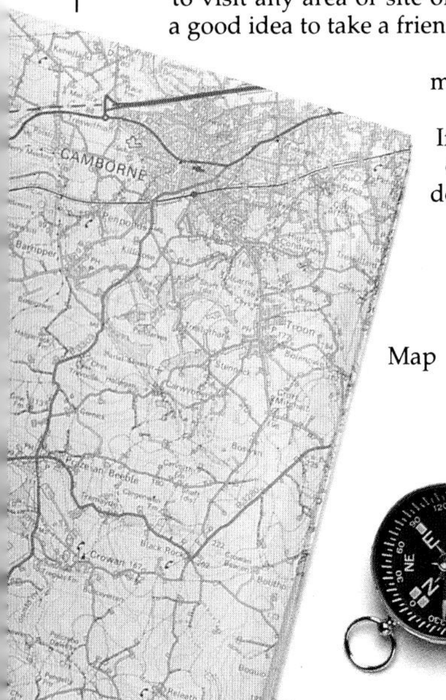

Map

Compass

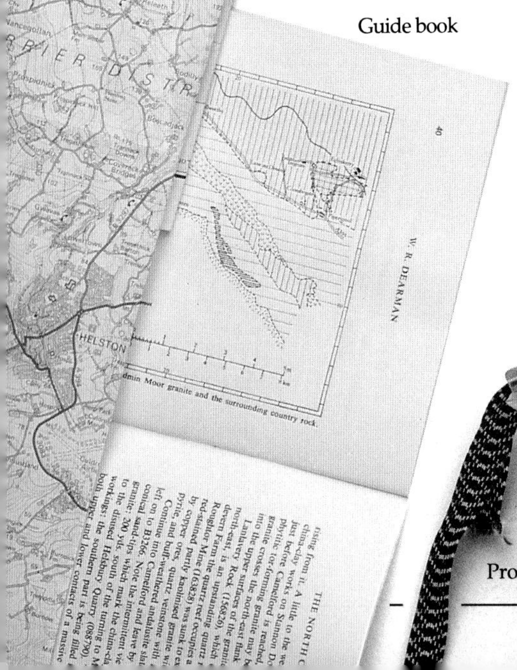

Guide book

PROTECTIVE CLOTHING
Great care must be taken when hammering rocks to prevent injury from flying rock and metal splinters. Wear protective goggles, a safety helmet, gloves, sturdy shoes or boots, and strong, waterproof clothing.

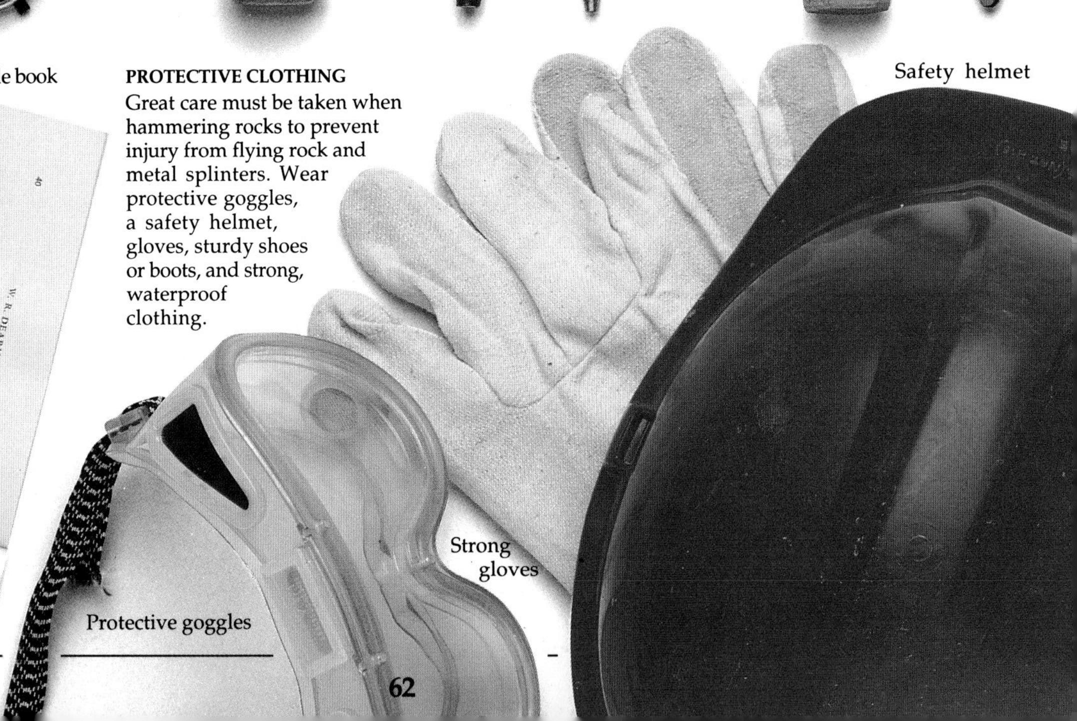

Safety helmet

Strong gloves

Protective goggles

RECORDING A FIND

The exact location and details of a find should be recorded in a notebook, and the specimen carefully numbered using a pen or sticky tape. A photograph or sketch of the specimen before collection will provide a permanent field record.

Notebook

Pencil

Pen

IDENTIFICATION

Specimens may be examined in the field with a x10 magnification hand lens. Indoors, a binocular microscope will reveal other details.

Camera to record site or location of find; when taking photographs try to give some indication of scale

Spatulas for fine work, such as cutting around fossils

Surgical knife for fine preparatory work on fossils

Palette knife for excavating small crystals from soft fossils or minerals

TOOLS FOR FINE WORK

Surplus rock can be removed from a specimen by washing in water and scrubbing lightly with a soft brush. Soft rock such as clay may be dug with a trowel, then sifted for small crystals or rock fragments.

Trowel for digging soft rocks

Sieve for sorting material

Paintbrushes for cleaning specimens

Muslin bag

Newspaper

TRANSPORTING SPECIMENS

Each specimen should be individually wrapped in newspaper or other protective material to prevent chipping or scratching. Crystal groups are usually very fragile and should be packed in tubes or boxes with suitable wrapping and carried in special collecting bags.

Plastic tube

Bubble wrap

Sealable plastic bag

KEEPING THE COLLECTION

To avoid damage to specimens, they should be stored in individual trays or boxes within a cabinet of shallow drawers. Some minerals fall apart rapidly in damp conditions, at high temperatures, or under the effects of light, so the needs of each one must be considered when organizing the collection.

Cardboard boxes for storing specimens

Labels for documenting specimens

Index

Acknowledgments

Dorling Kindersley would like to thank:
Dr Wendy Kirk of University College London; the staff of the British Museum (Natural History); and Gavin Morgan, Nick Merryman, and Christine Jones at the Museum of London for their advice and invaluable help in providing specimens.
Redland Brick Company and Jacobson Hirsch for the loan of equipment.
Anne-Marie Bulat for her work on the initial stages of the book.
David Nixon for design assistance, and Tim Hammond for editorial assistance.
Fred Ford and Mike Pilley of Radius Graphics, and Ray Owen and Nick Madren for artwork.

Picture credits
t= top b=bottom m=middle l=left r=right

Didier Barrault/Robert Harding Picture Libary: 37mr
Bridgeman Art Library/Bonhams, London: 55mr
Paul Brierley: 49b; 51m;
British Museum (Natural History): 42m; 43
N. A. Callow/Robert Harding Picture Library: 13b
G. & P. Corrigan/Robert Harding Picture Library: 23t
Diamond Information Centre: 60m
C. M. Dixon/Photoresources: 11b; 14t; 15t; 19b; 32b
Earth Satellite Corporation/Science Photo Library: 7t
Mary Evans Picture Library: 6t; 8; 9m; 12b; 15b; 16tl; 19t; 25; 26b; 28b; 30bl; 31b; 32t; 34t, ml; 36t; 37t, bl; 39b; 40t; 41t; 44tr; 50tr, br; 56mr; 57m; 58tl, tr; 59tl, b; 62t, m
Clive Friend/Woodmansterne Ltd.: 15m; 36b

Jon Gardey/Robert Harding Picture Library: 40b
Geoscience Features: 18t
Mike Gray/University College London: 17; 20tr; 24tr
Ian Griffiths/Robert Harding Picture Library: 13t
Robert Harding Picture Library: 13m; 18br; 21; 22bl; 23m; 27t, b; 35t, b; 56t; 59m
Brian Hawkes/Robert Harding Picture Library: 12m
Michael Holford: 50tl, bl; 51t; 54t, mr; 55t, ml
Glenn I. Huss: 40m
The Hutchinson Library: 35m; 51b; 56ml
Yoram Lehmann/Robert Harding Picture Library: 37ml
Kenneth Lucas/Planet Earth: 39t
Johnson Matthey: 58bl
Museum of London: 28t; 32m; 61tl, br
NASA: 41br
NASA/Robert Harding Picture Library: 6-7; 7b
NASA/Spectrum Colour Library: 11t
National Coal Board: 37br
Walter Rawlings/Robert Harding

Picture Library: 26m; 33b
John G. Ross/Robert Harding Picture Library: 53
K. Scholz/ZEFA: 10b
Nicholas Servian/Woodmansterne: 34mr
A. Sorrell/Museum of London: 29t
Spectrum Colour Library: 10m
R. F. Symes: 9tr
A. C. Waltham/Robert Harding Picture Library: 22br
Werner Forman Archive: 29b; 30br; 31tl, ml; 52t, b; 55b; 61m
G. M. Wilkins/Robert Harding Picture Library: 47
Woodmansterne : 58br
ZEFA: 16tr
Zeiss: 41bl
Reproduced with the permission of the Controller of Her Majesty's Stationery Office, Crown copyright: 54ml

Illustrations: Andrew Macdonald
6m, b; 14ml; 18bl; 22ml; 28mr; 30mr.

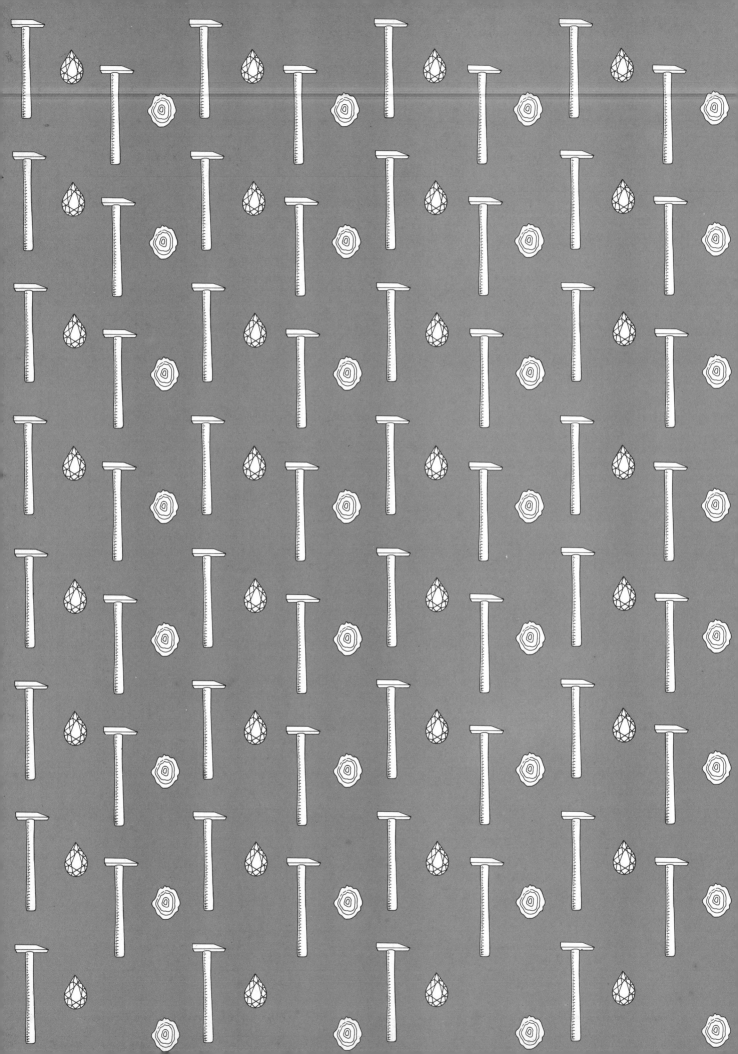